010
YO
Yonkers, N.Y.
Public Library.
Children's Services

A guide to subjects
& concepts in
picture book format

DATE			
3-24-22			

Non-Circulating

© THE BAKER & TAYLOR CO.

a guide to
subjects
& concepts in
picture book format

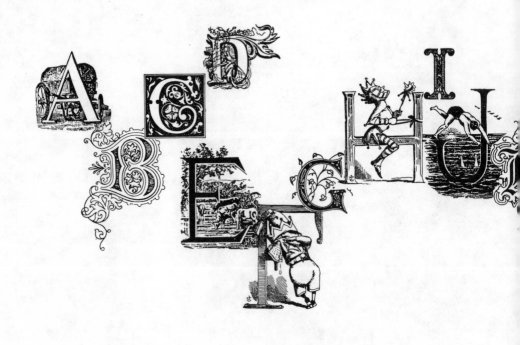

a guide to subjects & concepts in picture book format

Yonkers Public Library Children's Services 2nd. Edition

1979 OCEANA PUBLICATIONS, INC. DOBBS FERRY, NEW YORK

Library of Congress Cataloging in Publication Data

Yonkers, N.Y. Public Library. Children's Services.
  A guide to subjects & concepts in picture book format.

  Bibliography: p.
  1. Picture books for children--Indexes. 2. Children's
stories--Indexes. 3. Subject headings, Children's Literature.
  I. Title.
Z1037.Y65   1979   028.52   78-31811
SBN 0-379-20276-X

Manufactured in the United States of America

The illustrations on pages 23, 29, 63, 92, 108, 110, 150, 153 were reproduced by permission of Morgan and Morgan Publishing Inc., Dobbs Ferry, New York

contents

preface

Over the years, children's librarians at the Yonkers Public Library have received an increasing number of requests from parents, teachers, and library school students for books dealing with particular subjects, ideas, or themes on a preschool or early primary school level. The *Guide to Subjects and Concepts in Picture Book Format* evolved from the need to supplement the card catalog when handling such requests. It is not a buying guide; it is a "finding tool" for material for the younger child.

The selection and organization of the headings and subheadings used in the guide grew out of and hence reflect the types of requests we have received. Wherever possible, the wording of headings has been based on the standard forms appearing in *Sears List of Subject Headings*, 9th Edition (Wilson, 1965). Complete adherence to Sears, however, was impossible. It should be remembered, too, that, in many cases, the heading may not represent the *main* theme of a book but may have been assigned to call attention to a particular concept requested by patrons. Changes, additions, and expansions in headings used in the first edition reflect changing emphasis of patron requests (i.e. Male/Female Roles; Family Relations - Divorce or Single Parent Families), as well as changes in the types of books being published.

The guide has been limited to titles specifically classified as "picture book" in the Yonkers Public Library. There is other material which might be useful with the same age group, either classified as "easy books" or assigned Dewey Decimal Numbers. The cut-off date for inclusion of titles was October 1978. The great majority of titles included were listed in the 1977 *Books in Print*. However, some out-of-print books have been included (labeled "o.p.") since we felt many libraries would continue to hold copies for some time, or because material on the subjects covered by these books is hard to find.

It would be impossible to acknowledge properly all those who assisted in the preparation of the guide. The project began about fifteen years ago in the Children's Department of the Will Library. Almost everyone who has worked in this department has contributed in some way. As the project evolved, the children's librarians in the other four branches and the bookmobiles also participated, suggesting headings and examining titles. During the past year, the supervision of the guide in its final format has been the responsibility of JoAnne Roche, Children's Librarian at Will Library.

Madalynne Schoenfeld
Coordinator of Children's Services
November 1978

directions for use

The text of this guide is divided into 55 main subject categories which appear in upper case letters, e.g., ANIMALS. Main headings are subdivided when there are two or more titles representing a subheading, e.g., ANIMALS - Bears. The "General" subheading, when it is used, includes comprehensive works about the subject. The "Other" category includes subjects for which there was only one representative title. Titles in the "Other" category have the subject added in parentheses after the entry unless the title is self-explanatory.

There is a LIST OF HEADINGS in an outline format on the following pages. A "See Reference" directs the user to the correct main heading for some widely-asked-for subjects that do not appear as headings, e.g. Witches - See HOLIDAYS - Halloween. A "See Also Reference" guides the user to other main headings that contain material related to a particular subject, e.g., RELIGIOUS STORIES - See Also HOLIDAYS.

list of
headings

a guide to
subjects
& concepts in
picture book format

a

ALPHABET BOOKS

Alexander, Anne. ABC of cars and trucks. Doubleday 1971.

Anglund, Joan Walsh. In a pumpkin shell. Harcourt 1960.

Anno, Mitsumasa. Anno's alphabet. Crowell 1975.

Baskin, Leonard. Hosie's alphabet. Viking 1972.

Brown, Marcia. All butterflies. Scribner 1974.

Brown, Marcia. Peter Piper's alphabet. Scribner 1959.

Burningham, John. ABC. Bobbs-Merrill 1964.

Carle, Eric. All about Arthur. Watts 1974.

Cooney, Barbara. A garland of games and other diversions. Holt, 1969.

Crews, Donald. We read: A to Z. Harper & Row 1967.

Delaunay, Sonia. Alphabet. Crowell 1970.

Duvoisin, Roger. A for the ark. Lothrop, Lee & Shepard 1952.

Eichenberg, Fritz. Ape in a cape. Harcourt 1973.

Falls, C.B. ABC book Doubleday 1957.

Gag, Wanda. ABC bunny. Coward-McCann 1933.

Garten, Jan. The alphabet tale. Random 1964.

Greenaway, Kate. A apple pie. Warne n.d.

Gretz, Susanna. Teddybears abc. Follett 1975.

Grossbart, Francine. A big city. Harper & Row 1966.

Hefter, Richard.　The great big alphabet picture book with lots of words. Grosset 1972.

Howard-Gibbon, Amelia Frances.　An illustrated comic alphabet. Walck 1966.

Ilsley, Velma.　M is for moving.　Walck 1966.

Ipcar, Dahlov.　I love my anteater with an A.　Knopf 1964.

Jacobs, Leland B.　Alphabet of girls.　Holt 1969.

Johnson, Crockett.　Harold's ABC.　Harper & Row 1963.

Lear, Edward.　ABC.　McGraw 1965.

Lear, Edward.　Edward Lear's a nonsense alphabet.　Doubleday 1962.

Lord, Beman.　Our new baby's ABC.　Walck 1964.

McGinley, Phyllis L.　All around the town.　Lippincott 1948.

Matthiesen, Thomas.　ABC; an alphabet book.　Platt & Munk 1966.

Mendoza, George.　The alphabet boat.　McGraw 1972.

Miles, Miska.　Apricot ABC.　Little, Brown 1969.

Munari, Bruno.　ABC.　World Pub., 1960.

Newberry, Clare.　The kitten's ABC.　Harper & Row 1965.

Ogle, Lucille.　A B See.　McGraw-Hill 1973.

Oxenbury, Helen.　Helen Oxenbury's ABC of things.　Watts 1972.

Piatti, Celestino.　Celestino Piatti's animal ABC.　Atheneum 1966.

Polak, Johan.　True to life ABC book including numbers.　Grosset & Dunlap 1962.

Rey, H. A.　Curious George learns the alphabet.　Houghton 1963.

Rockwell, Anne.　Albert B. Cub & Zebra: an alphabet storybook. Crowell 1977.

Rojankovsky, Feodor. F. Rojankovsky's ABC. Golden Press 1970.

Ruben, Patricia. Apples to zippers. Doubleday 1976.

Schoolfield, Lucille D. Sounds the letters make. Little, Brown 1940.

Sendak, Maurice. Alligators all around. Harper 1962.

The Sesame Street book of letters. NAL 1971.

Seuss, Dr. Dr. Seuss's ABC. Random House 1963.

Shuttlesworth, Dorothy. ABC of buses. Doubleday 1965.

Tudor, Tasha. A is for Annabelle. Walck 1954.

Walker, Barbara. I packed my trunk. Follett 1969.

Watson, Nancy. What does A begin with? Knopf 1956.

Wildsmith, Brian. ABC. Watts 1962.

Wondriska, William. A long piece of string. Holt 1963.

Aulaire, Ingri d'. Animals everywhere. Doubleday 1954.

Bannon, Laura. Little people of the night. Houghton 1963.

Falls, C.B. ABC book. Doubleday 1957.

Fisher, Aileen. Do bears have mothers, too? Crowell 1973.

Gay, Zhenya. Look. Viking 1952.

Gay, Zhenya. The nicest time of year. Viking 1960.

Ipcar, Dahlov. Bright barnyard. Knopf 1966.

Ipcar, Dahlov. Brown cow farm. Doubleday 1959.

Ipcar, Dahlov. I like animals. Knopf 1960.

Ipcar, Dahlov. Wild and tame animals. Doubleday 1962.

Provensen, Alice. Our animal friends at Maple Hill Farm. Random 1974.

Rojankovsky, Feodor. Animals on the farm. Knopf 1967.

Schwartz, Elizabeth. When animals are babies. Holiday 1964.

Selsam, Millicent. All kinds of babies. Four Winds 1967.

Simon, Mina. If you were an eel, how would you feel? Follett 1963.

Slobodkin, Louis. The friendly animals. Vanguard n.d.

Supraner, Robyn. Would you rather be a tiger? Houghton 1973.

Tresselt, Alvin. Under the trees and through the grass. Lothrop 1962.

Webb, Clifford. More animals from everywhere. Warne 1959.

Webb, Clifford. Strange creatures. Warne 1964.

Wildsmith, Brian. Brian Wildsmith's wild animals. Watts 1967.

Wildsmith, Brian. Python's party. Watts 1974.

Ylla. Animal babies. Harper 1959.

ANIMALS *Bears*

Alexander, Martha. And my mean old mother will be sorry, blackboard bear. Dial 1972.

Alexander, Martha. The blackboard bear. Dial 1969.

Barr, Cathrine. Bears in-bears out. Walck 1967.

Binzen, Bill. Alfred the little bear. Doubleday 1970.

Bishop, Claire. Twenty-two bears. Viking 1964.

Bright, Robert. Friendly bear. Doubleday 1957.

Bright, Robert. Me and the bears. Doubleday 1951.

Craft, Ruth. The winter bear. Atheneum 1974.

Du Bois, William Pene. Bear party. Viking 1951.

Fatio, Louise. The happy lion and the bear. McGraw 1964.

Flack, Marjorie. Ask Mr. Bear. Macmillan 1958.

Flora, James. Sherwood walks home. Harcourt 1966.

Freeman, Don. Beady bear. Viking 1954.

Freeman, Don. Bearymore. Viking 1976.

Freeman, Don. Corduroy. Viking 1968.

Ginsburg, Mirra. Two greedy bears. Macmillan 1976.

Gretz, Susanna. Teddybears abc. Follett 1975.

Hayes, Geoffrey. Bear by himself. Harper 1976.

Janice. Little bear's pancake party. Lothrop 1960. (and other books in the series)

Lipkind, William. Nubber bear. Harcourt 1966.

McCloskey, Robert. Blueberries for Sal. Viking 1948.

Marino, Dorothy. Buzzy bear's busy day. Watts 1965. (and other books in the series) o.p.

Monsell, Helen Albee. Paddy's Christmas. Knopf 1924, 1942.

Neumann, Rudolf. The bad bear. Macmillan 1967.

Ormondroyd, Edward. Theodore. Parnassus 1966.

Ormondroyd, Edward. Theodore's rival. Parnaussus 1971.

Ressner, Phil. August explains. Harper 1963.

Robinson, Barbara. The fattest bear in the first grade. Random 1969.

Rockwell, Anne. Head to toe. Doubleday 1973.

Sharmat, Marjorie. I'm terrific. Holiday 1977.

Skorpen, Liesel Moak. Outside my window. Harper 1968.

Trent, Robbie. Cubby's world. Abingdon 1966.

Turkle, Brinton. Deep in the forest. Dutton 1976.

Van Stockum, Hilda. Little old bear. Viking 1962.

Ward, Lynd Kendall. The biggest bear. Houghton 1952.

Ylla. Polar bear brothers. Harper 1960.

Ylla. Two little bears. Harper 1954.

ANIMALS *Camel*

Freschet, Berniece. The happy dromedary. Scribner 1977.

Goodenow, Earle. The last camel. Walck 1968.

Tworkov. Jack. The camel who took a walk. Aladdin 1951.

ANIMALS *Cat*

Averill, Esther. Jenny's birthday book. Harper 1954. (and other books in the series)

Brenner, Barbara. Cunningham's rooster. Parent's Mag. Press 1975.

Brown, Marcia. Felice. Scribner 1958.

Brown, Margaret W. A Pussycat's Christmas. Crowell 1949.

Bulla, Clyde Robert. The Valentine cat. Crowell 1959.

Calhoun, Mary. Wobble the witch cat. Morrow 1958.

Carroll, Ruth. The Christmas kitten. Walck 1970.

Chalmers, Mary. Be good, Harry. Harper 1967.

Clymer, Eleanor. Horatio. Atheneum 1968. (and other books in the series)

De Regniers, Beatrice Schenk. Cats, Cats, Cats, Cats, Cats... Pantheon 1958.

Flack, Marjorie. Angus and the cat. Doubleday 1971.

Flory, Jane. We'll have a friend for lunch. Houghton 1974.

Francoise. Minou. Scribner 1962.

Gag, Wanda. Millions of cats. Coward 1928.

Ginsburg, Mirra. Three kittens. Crown 1973.

Holl, Adelaide.   One kitten for Kim.   Addison-Wesley 1969.

Holmes, Efner Tudor.   The Christmas cat.   Crowell 1976.

Johnston, Johanna.   Sugarplum and Snowball.   Knopf 1968.

Keats, Ezra Jack.   Hi, Cat!   Macmillan 1970.

Keats, Ezra Jack.   Kitten for a day.   Watts 1974.

Kerr, Judith.   Mog, the forgetful cat.   Parent's Mag. Press 1972.

Kerr, Judith.   When Willy went to the wedding.   Parent's Mag. Press 1973.

Knotts, Howard.   The winter cat.   Harper 1972.

Longman, Harold S.   The castle of a thousand cats.   Addison-Wesley 1972.

Martin, Patricia Miles.   That cat! 1-2-3.   Putnam 1969.

Newberry, Clare T.   April's kittens.   Harper 1940.

Newberry, Clare T.   The kitten's ABC.   Harper 1965.

Newberry, Clare T.   Mittens.   Harper 1936.

Newberry, Clare T.   Widget.   Harper 1958.

Northrup, Mili.   The watch cat.   Bobbs-Merrill 1968.

Peet, Bill.   Jennifer and Josephine.   Houghton 1967.

Peppe, Rodney.   Cat and mouse.   Holt 1973.

Potter, Beatrix.   The roly-poly pudding.   Warne 1936.

Potter, Beatrix.   The story of Miss Moppet.   Warne 1904.

Potter, Beatrix.   The tale of Tom Kitten.   Warne 1935.

Robinson, Tom.   Buttons.   Viking 1938.

Ross, G. Max.   When Lucy went away.   Dutton 1976.

Schatz, Letta. Whiskers, my cat. McGraw 1967.

Seredy, Kate. Gypsy. Viking 1951.

Skaar, Grace. The very little dog and the smart little kitty. Young
    Scott Bks. 1947.

Stewart, Elizabeth. Kim the kitten. Reilly and Lee 1961.

Sylvester, Natalie. Summer on Cleo's island. Farrar 1977.

Thayer, Jane. The cat that joined the club. Morrow 1967.

Thayer, Jane. I'm not a cat, said Emerald. Morrow 1970.

Thayer, Jane. The outside cat. Morrow 1957.

Turner, Nancy. When it rained cats and dogs. Lippincott 1946.

Udry, Janice. Oh no, cat! Coward 1976.

Waber, Bernard. Good-bye, funny dumpy-lumpy. Houghton 1977.

Will. Russet and the two reds. Harcourt 1962.

Will. The two reds. Harcourt 1950.

Williams, Gweniera. Timid Timothy. Scott 1944.

Williams, Jay. Pettifur. Four Winds 1977.

Wright, Dare. Doll and the kitten. Doubleday 1960.

Yashima, Taro. Momo's kitten. Viking 1961.

Yeoman, John. Mouse trouble. Macmillan 1972.

ANIMALS *Cow*

Hoff, Syd. Roberto and the bull. McGraw 1969.

Jewell, Nancy. Calf, goodnight. Harper 1973.

Krasilovsky, Phyllis. Cow who fell in the canal. Doubleday 1957.

9

Leaf, Munro.   The story of Ferdinand.   Viking 1936.

Lent, Blaire.   Pistachio.   Little 1964.

ANIMALS *Deer*

Bemelmans, Ludwig.   Parsley.   Harper 1955.

Carrick, Donald.   The deer in the pasture.   Greenwillow 1976.

ANIMALS *Dog*

Alexander, Martha.   Bobo's dream.   Dial 1970.

Ardizzone, Edward.   Tim's friend Towser.   Walck 1962.

Aulaire, Ingri d'.   Foxie, the singing dog.   Doubleday 1969.

Bettina.   Pantaloni.   Harper 1957.

Carrick, Carol.   The foundling.   Seabury 1977.

Carroll, Ruth.   What Whiskers did.   Walck 1965.

Christian, Mary B.   No dogs allowed, Jonathan!   Addison-Wesley 1975.

Coatsworth, Elizabeth.   The fox friend.   Macmillan 1966.

Du Bois, William Pene.   Otto at sea.   Viking 1958.   (and other books
    in the series)

Flack, Marjorie.   Angus and the ducks.   Doubleday 1939. (and other
    books in the series)

Freeman, Don.   Ski pup.   Viking 1963.

Gag, Wanda.   Nothing at all.   Coward 1941.

Grabianski, Janusz.   Dogs.   Watts 1968.   o.p.

Graham, Margaret Bloy.   Benjy and the barking bird.   Harper 1971.

Graham, Margaret. Benjy's boat trip. Harper 1977.

Gramatky, Hardie.   Happy's Christmas.   Putnam 1970.

Hoff, Syd. Lengthy. Putnam 1964.

Hurd, Edith. Little dog, dreaming. Harper 1967.

Hurlimann, Bettina. Barry: the story of a brave St. Bernard. Harcourt.
    1967.

Kahl, Virginia. Maxie. Scribner 1956.

Keats, Ezra Jack. Kitten for a day. Watts 1974.

Keats, Ezra Jack. Skates! Watts 1973.

Keats, Ezra Jack. Whistle for Willie. Viking 1964.

Kroll, Steven. Is Milton missing? Holiday 1975.

Lathrop, Dorothy. Puppies for keeps. Macmillan 1943.

Leaf, Munro. Noodle. Four Winds 1965.

Lenski, Lois. A dog came to school. Walck 1955.

Nakatani, Chiyoko. The day Chiro was lost. World 1969.

Nodset, Joan L. Go away, dog. Harper 1963.

Peet, Bill.   The whingdingdilly.   Houghton 1970.

Potter, Beatrix. The pie and the patty pan. Warne 1905.

Rey, Margret. Pretzel. Harper 1944.

Rowand, Phyllis. George. Little, Brown 1956.

Sharmat, Marjorie. Morris Brookside, a dog. Holiday House 1973.

Skaar, Grace. The very little dog and the smart little kitty. Young
    Scott Bks., 1947

Skorpen, Liesel Moak. All the lassies. Dial 1970.

Skorpen, Liesel. Old Arthur. Harper 1972.

Stewart, Elizabeth. Billy buys a dog. Reilly & Lee 1950.

Tudor, Tasha. Corgiville fair. Crowell 1971.

Turkle, Brinton, The sky dog. Viking 1969.

Turner, Nancy Byrd. When it rained cats and dogs. Lippincott 1946. o.p.

Weil, Lisl. Shivers. Houghton 1967.

Welch, Martha McKeen. Just like puppies. Coward 1969.

Welch, Martha McKeen. Pudding and pie. Coward 1968.

Will. Finders keepers. Harcourt 1951.

Zion, Gene. Harry, the dirty dog. Harper 1956. (And other books in the series)

ANIMALS *Donkey*

Duvoisin, Roger. Donkey-donkey. Parents Mag., 1940, 1968.

Francoise. Chouchou. Scribner 1958.

Palazzo, Tony. Bianco and the new world. Viking 1957.

Showalter, Jean B. The donkey ride. Doubleday 1967. o.p.

Steig, William. Farmer Palmer's wagon ride. Farrar 1974.

Steig, William. Sylvester and the magic pebble. Dutton 1973.

Thompson, Vivian L. Keola's Hawaiian donkey. Golden Gate 1966.

ANIMALS *Elephant*

Brunhoff, Jean de. The story of Babar. Random 1960, ^{C}1937. (And other books in the series)

Ets, Marie H. Elephant in a well. Viking 1972.

Joslin, Sesyle. Brave baby elephant. Harcourt 1960. (And other books
   in the series)

Peet, Bill. Ella. Houghton 1964.

Petersham, Maud. Circus baby. Macmillan 1950.

Quigley, Lillian. The blind men and the elephant. Scribner 1959.

Schlein, Mariam. Elephant herd. Scott 1954.

Seuss, Dr. Horton hatches the egg. Random 1940.

Simon, Norma. Elly the elephant. St. Martins 1962.

Vipont, Elfrida. The elephant and the bad baby. Coward 1969.

Wahl, Jan. Hello elephant. Holt 1964.

Will. Chaga. Harcourt 1955.

Ylla. The little elephant. Harper 1956.

ANIMALS *Fox*

Aldridge, Josephine. Reasons and raisins. Parnassus 1971.

Coatsworth, Elizabeth. The fox friend. Macmillan 1966.

Domanska, Janina. The best of the bargain. Greenwillow 1977.

The fox went out on a chilly night. Illus. by Peter Spier. Doubleday
   1961.

Hogrogian, Nonny. One fine day. Macmillan 1971.

Miles, Miska. Fox and the fire. Little 1966.

Potter, Beatrix. The tale of Mr. Tod. Warner 1939.

13

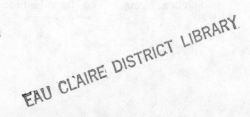

ANIMALS *Goat*

Asbjornsen, Peter.   The three Billy goats gruff; illus. by Marcia Brown. Harcourt 1957.

Galdone, Paul.   The three Billy goats gruff.   Seabury 1973.

Slobodkin, Louis.   The polka-dot goat.   Macmillan 1964.

Weil, Lisl.   The hopping knapsack.   Macmillan 1970.

Will.   Billy the Kid.   Harcourt.   1961.

ANIMALS *Groundhog*

Cohen, Carol.   Wake up, groundhog.   Crown 1975.

Kesselman, Wendy.   Time for Jody.   Harper 1975.

Wiese, Kurt.   The groundhog and his shadow.   Viking 1959.

ANIMALS *Hippopotamus*

Brown, Marcia.   How, Hippo!   Scribner 1969.

Duvoisin, Roger.   Veronica.   Knopf 1961.

Kishida, Eriko.   The hippo boat.   World 1967.

Kishida, Eriko.   Hippopotamus.   Prentice-Hall 1963.

Mahy, Margaret.   The boy who was followed home.   Watts 1975.

Marshall, James.   George and Martha.   Houghton 1972.   (And other books in series)

Parker, Nancy W.   Love from Uncle Clyde.   Dodd 1977.

Schlein, Miriam.   Heavy is a hippopotamus.   Scott 1954.

Standon, Anna.   The Hippo had hiccups.   Coward 1964.

14

ANIMALS *Horse*

Anderson, Clarence William. Billy and Blaze. Macmillan 1962.

Anderson, Clarence William. Lonesome little colt. Macmillan 1961.

Dennis, Wesley. Flip. Viking 1941. (And other books in the series)

Ipcar, Dahlov. One horse farm. Doubleday 1950.

Ipcar, Dahlov. World full of horses. Doubleday 1955.

Keeping, Charles. Molly o' the Moors. World 1966.

Krauss, Ruth. Charlotte and the white horse. Harper 1955.

McGinley, Phyllis. The horse who lived upstairs. Lippincott 1944.

Reid, Barbara. Miguel and his racehorse. Morrow 1973.

Schick, Eleanor. Jeanie goes riding. Macmillan 1968.

Skaar, Grace. A boy and his horse. Scott 1958.

Slobodkin, Louis. Picco, the sad Italian pony. Vanguard 1961.

Steiner, Alexis. All my horses. Lerner 1965.

Thayer, Jane. Horse with the Easter bonnet. Morrow 1953.

Will. Even Steven. Harcourt 1952.

Wright, Dare. Look at a colt. Random 1969.

Zolotow, Charlotte. I have a horse of my own. Abelard-Schuman
    1964.

ANIMALS *Kangaroo*

Payne, Emmy. Katy no-pocket. Houghton 1944.

Ungerer, Tomi. Adelaide. Harper 1959.

ANIMALS *Lion*

Adamson, Joy. Elsa. Pantheon 1963.

Daugherty, James. Andy and the lion. Viking 1970.

Fatio, Louise. The happy lion. McGraw 1954. (And other books in the series)

Freeman, Don. Dandelion. Viking 1964.

La Fontaine. The lion and the rat. Watts 1963.

Peet, Bill. Hubert's hair-raising adventure. Houghton 1959.

Peet, Bill. Randy's dandy lions. Houghton 1964.

Purdy, Susan. If you have a yellow lion. Lippincott 1966.

Sendak, Maurice. Pierre. Harper 1962.

ANIMALS *Llama*

Eiseman, Alberta. Candido. Macmillan 1967.

Rockwell, Anne. The good llama. World 1968.

ANIMALS *Mole*

Chorao, Kay. Maudie's umbrella. Dutton 1975.

Hoban, Russell. The mole family's Christmas. Parents' Mag. Pr. 1969.

ANIMALS *Monkey*

Booz, Elizabeth. Josephine. Houghton 1962.

Goodall, John S. Jacko. Harcourt 1972.

Kepes, Juliet. Five little monkeys. Houghton 1952.

Kepes, Juliet. Run, little monkeys! Run, run, run! Pantheon 1974.

Knight, Hilary. Where's Wallace? Harper 1964.

Kravetz, Nathan. A monkey's tale. Little 1964.

Rey, H.A. Cecily G and the 9 monkeys. Houghton 1942.

Rey, Hans A. & Margaret. Curious George. Houghton 1941. (And other books in the series)

Rietveld, Jane. Monkey Island. Viking 1963.

Slobodkina, Esphyr. Caps for sale. Scott 1947.

Suba, Susanne. The monkeys and the pedlar. Viking 1970.

Wolkstein, Diane. The cool ride in the sky. Knopf 1973.

ANIMALS *Moose*

McNeer, May. My friend Mac. Houghton 1960.

Seuss, Dr. Thidwick, the big-hearted moose. Random 1948.

ANIMALS *Mouse*

Brown, Marcia. One a mouse... Scribner 1961.

Carle, Eric. Do you want to be my friend? Crowell 1971.

Fisher, Aileen. Sing, little mouse. Crowell 1969.

Freeman, Don. The guard mouse. Viking 1967.

Freeman, Don. Norman the doorman. Viking 1959.

Freeman, Don. Pet of the Met. Viking 1953.

Gag, Wanda. Snippy and Snappy. Coward 1931.

Harris, Dorothy, Joan. The house mouse. Warne 1973.

Harris, Leon A. The great picture robbery. Atheneum 1963.

Helps, Racey. Mr. Roley to the rescue. Chilton 1966.

Lionni, Leo. Alexander and the wind-up mouse. Pantheon 1969.

Lionni, Leo. Frederick. Pantheon 1967.

Lionni, Leo. Theodore and the talking mushroom. Pantheon 1971.

Ormondroyd, Edward. Broderick. Parnassus 1969.

Peppe, Rodney. Cat and mouse. Holt 1973.

Potter, Beatrix. The tailor of Gloucester. Warne 1903, 1931.

Potter, Beatrix. The tale of Johnny town-mouse. Warne 1946, 1918.

Potter, Beatrix. The tale of Mrs. Tittlemouse. Warne 1910.

Potter, Beatrix. The tale of two bad mice. Warne 1904, 1932.

Rand, Ann. So small. Harcourt 1962.

Roach, Marilynne K. The mouse and the song. Parents' Mag. Pr. 1974.

Steig, William. Amos & Boris. Farrar 1971.

Titus, Eve. Anatole. McGraw 1956. (And other books in the series)

Warren, Joyce. A mouse to be free. See Cliff 1973.

Wells, Rosemary. Noisy Nora. Dial 1973.

Yeoman, John. Mouse trouble. Macmillan 1972.

Zion, Gene. The sugar mouse cake. Scribner 1964.

ANIMALS *Pig*

Goodall, John S. Adventures of Paddy Pork. Harcourt 1968 (And other books in the series)

Marshall, James. Yummers! Houghton 1972.

Oxenbury, Helen. Pig tale. Morrow 1973.

Potter, Beatrix. The tale of Little Pig Robinson. David McKay 1930.

Potter, Beatrix. The tale of pigling bland. Warne 1913, 1941.

Steig, William. The amazing bone. Farrar 1976.

Steig, William. Farmer Palmer's wagon ride. Farrar 1974.

Steig, William. Roland, the Minstrel Pig. Harper 1968.

Wondriska, William. Mr. Brown and Mr. Gray. Holt 1968.

ANIMALS *Rabbit*

Adams, Adrienne. The Easter egg artists. Scribner 1976.

Anderson, Lonzo. Two hundred rabbits. Viking 1968.

Becker, John. Seven little rabbits. Walker 1973.

Bright, Robert. My hopping bunny. Doubleday 1960.

Brown, Margaret W. The runaway bunny. Harper 1942.

Fatio, Louise. The happy lion's rabbits. McGraw 1974.

Fisher, Aileen. Listen, rabbit. Crowell 1964.

Friedrich, Priscilla. The Easter bunny that overslept. Lothrop 1957.

Heyward, Du Bose. Country bunny and the little gold shoes. Houghton 1939.

Hoban, Tana. Where is it? Macmillan 1974.

Kahl, Virginia. Habbits of rabbits. Scribner 1957.

Miles, Miska. Rabbit garden. Little 1967.

Newberry, Clare T. Marshmallow. Harper 1942.

Peet, Bill.   Huge Harold.   Houghton 1961.

Potter, Beatrix.   The story of a fierce bad rabbit.   Warne, n.d.

Potter, Beatrix.   The tale of Benjamin Bunny.   Warne 1904, 1932.

Potter, Beatrix.   The tale of the flopsy bunnies.   Warne 1909, 1937.

Potter, Beatrix.   The tale of Peter Rabbit.   Warne n.d.

Rey, Margret.   Spotty.   Harper 1945.

Schlein, Miriam.   The rabbit's world.   Four Winds 1973.

Skorpen, Liesel Moak.   Michael.   Harper 1975.

Wahl, Jan.   Doctor Rabbit.   Delacorte 1970.

Will.   Christmas Bunny.   Harcourt 1953.

Williams, Garth.   The rabbit's wedding.   Harper 1958.

Zolotow, Charlotte.   The bunny who found Easter.   Parnassus 1959.

Zolotow, Charlotte.   Mr. Rabbit and the lovely present.   Harper 1962.

ANIMALS *Raccoon*

Bourne, Miriam Anne.   Raccoons are for loving.   Random House 1968.

Dizick. Missy C.   Russle,   Simon and Schuster 1970.

Welch, Martha.   Just like puppies.   Coward 1969.

ANIMALS *Rhinoceros*

Ardizzone, Edward.   Diana and her rhinoceros.   Walck 1964. o.p.

Kipling, Rudyard.   How the rhinoceros got his skin.   Walker 1974.

ANIMALS *Sheep*

Francoise.   Jeanne-Marie counts her sheep.   Scribner 1957.

Peet, Bill. Buford the little bighorn. Houghton 1967.

ANIMALS *Skunk*

Schoenherr, John. The barn. Little 1968.

Stevens, Carla. Rabbit & skunk and the big fight. Young Scott Bks.,
1964.

ANIMALS *Squirrel*

Potter, Beatrix. The tale of squirrel Nutkin. Warne 1903, 1931.

Potter, Beatrix. The tale of Timmy Tiptoe. Warne 1911, 1939.

Robinson, Tom. Mr. Red Squirrel. Viking 1943.

Welch, Martha M. Nibbit. Coward 1969.

Wildsmith, Brian. Squirrels. Watts 1974.

Young, Miriam. Miss Suzy. Parents' Mag. Pr., 1964.

Zion, Gene. The meanest squirrel I ever met. Scribner 1962.

ANIMALS *Tiger*

Kerr, Judith. The tiger who came to tea. Coward 1968.

Sucksdorff, Astrid B. Chendru: the boy and the tiger. Harcourt 1960.

Taylor, Mark. Henry explores the jungle. Atheneum 1968.

Villarejo, Mary. Fuzzy the tiger. Knopf 1962. o.p.

Yurdin, Betty. The tiger in the teapot. Holt 1968.

ANIMALS *Whale*

Broger, Achim. Good morning, whale. Macmillan 1974.

Duvoisin, Roger. Christmas whale. Knopf 1945.

21

Hurd, Edith Thacher.   What whale? Where?   Harper 1966.

McCloskey, Robert.   Burt Dow, deep water man.   Viking 1963.

Steig, William.   Amos & Boris.   Farrar 1971.

ANIMALS *Wolf*

Allard, Harry.   It's so nice to have a wolf around the house.   Doubleday
1977.

Goble, Paul.   The friendly wolf.   Bradbury 1975.

Hoover, Helen.   Great wolf and the good woodsman.   Parents' Mag. Pr.
1967.

Prokofieff, Serge.   Peter and the wolf.   Knopf 1940.

Rockwell, Anne.   The wolf who had a wonderful dream.   Crowell 1973.

Steig, William.   The amazing bone.   Farrar 1976.

ANIMALS *Other*

Berson, Harold.   Henry possum.   Crown Pub. 1973. (opossum)

Borg, Inga.   Parrak- the white reindeer.   Warne 1959.

Carlson, Natalie Savage.   Marie Louise's heyday.   Scribner 1975.
(Mongoose)

Goodall, John S.   Shrewbettina's birthday.   Harcourt 1970 (Shrew)

Hoban, Russell.   Charlie the tramp.   Four Winds 1966 (Beaver)

Hoban, Russell.   Harvey's hideout.   Parents' Mag. 1969. (Muskrat)

Lindop, Edmund.   Pelorus Jack: Dolphin pilot.   Little 1964.

Miller, Edna.   Pebbles; a pack rat.   Prentice-Hall 1976.

Rey, Hans Augusto.   Cecily G and the 9 monkeys.   Houghton 1942.
(Giraffe)

Schweitzer, Byrd Baylor. Amigo. Macmillan 1963. (Prairie dog)

Thayer, Jane. A drink for little red diker. Marrow 1963 (Antelope)

Ungerer, Tomi. Rufus. Harper 1961 (Bat)

b

BABIES

Borack, Barbara. Someone small. Harper & Row 1969.

Brown, Myra Berry. Amy and the new baby. Watts 1965. o.p.

Chaffin, Lillie D. Tommy's big problem. Lantern 1965.

Hoban, Russell. A baby sister for Frances. Harper & Row 1964.

Holland, Viki. We are having a baby. Scribner 1972.

Jarrell, Mary. The knee baby. Farrar 1973.

Keats, Ezra Jack. Peter's chair. Harper & Row 1967.

Lord, Beman. Our new baby's ABC. Walck 1964.

Mann, Peggy. That new baby. Coward 1967.

Ness, Evaline. Yeck eck. Dutton 1974.

Schick, Eleanor. Peggy's new brother. Macmillan 1970.

Scott, Ann Herbert. On mother's lap. McGraw 1972.

Vigna, Judith. Couldn't we have a turtle instead? Whitman 1975.

Wasson, Valentina P.   The chosen baby. Lippincott 1977. (Adoption)

BIRDS *General*

Conklin, Gladys.   If I were a bird.   Holiday 1965.

Flack, Marjorie.   The restless robin.   Houghton 1937.

Grabianski, Janusz.   Birds.   Watts 1968.

Hawkinson, Lucy.   Birds in the sky.   Childrens' 1965.

Holl, Adelaide.   The remarkable egg.   Lothrop 1968.

Ipcar, Dahlov.   Bright barnyard.   Knopf 1966.

Ipcar, Dahlov.   The song of the day birds and the night birds.   Doubleday 1967.

Lionni, Leo.   Tico and the golden wings.   Pantheon 1964.

Peet, Bill.   The pinkish, purplish, bluish egg.   Houghton 1963.

Skorpen, Liesel Moak.   Bird.   Harper & Row 1976.

Stiles, Martha B.   Dougal looks for birds.   Scholastic 1972.

Valentin, Ursula.   Her Minkepatt and his friends.   Braziller 1965.

Wildsmith, Brian.   Brian Wildsmith's birds.   Watts 1967.

BIRDS *Chicken*

Aulaire, Ingri d'.   Don't count your chicks.   Doubleday 1973.

Brenner, Barbara.   Cunningham's rooster.   Parents' Mag. 1975.

Cooney, Barbara.   Chanticleer and the fox.   Crowell 1958.

Fatio, Louise.   Red bantam.   McGraw 1963.

Hader, Berta.   Cock-a-doodle-doo.   Macmillan 1939.

Hewett, Anita.   The little white hen.   McGraw 1962.

Lobel, Arnold.   How the rooster saved the day.   Greenwillow 1977.

Miles, Miska. Chicken forgets. Little, Brown 1976.

Provensen, Alice. My little hen. Random 1973.

Rockwell, Anne. The wonderful eggs of Furicchia. World Pub. 1969.

Sherman, Nancy. Gwendolyn the miracle hen. Golden 1961.

Watson, Nancy. Katie's chickens. Knopf 1965.

Will. The little tiny rooster. Harcourt 1960.

Williams, Garth. The chicken book. Delacorte 1970.

BIRDS *Dove*

Freeman, Don. The turtle and the dove. Viking 1964.

Potter, Beatrix. Tale of the faithful dove. Warne 1970.

BIRDS *Duck*

Conover, Chris. Six little ducks. Crowell 1976.

Duvoisin, Roger. Two lonely ducks. Knopf 1955.

Flack, Marjorie. Angus and the ducks. Doubleday 1939.

Flack, Marjorie. Story about Ping. Viking 1933.

McCloskey, Robert. Make way for ducklings. Viking 1941.

Potter, Beatrix. The tale of Jemima puddle-duck. Warne 1908.

Sewell, Helen Moore. Blue barns. Macmillan 1933.

Wildsmith, Brian. The little wood duck. Watts 1973.

BIRDS *Goose*

Duvoisin, Roger. Petunia. Knopf 1950. (And other books in the series)

Galdone, Joanna. Gertrude, the goose who forgot. Watts 1975.

Hader, Berta. Two is company, three's a crowd. Macmillan 1965.

Lasell, Fen. Fly away goose. Houghton 1965.

Massie, Diane Redfield. Briar Rose and the golden eggs. Parents' 1973.

Preston, Edna Mitchell. Squawk to the moon, little goose. Viking 1974.

Sandburg, Helga. Josel and the wild goose. Dial 1963.

BIRDS *Owl*

Hutchins, Pat. Good-night, owl! Macmillan 1972.

Kraus, Robert. Owliver. Windmill 1974.

Paitti, Celestino. The happy owls. Atheneum 1963.

Scharen, Beatrix. Tillo. Addison-Wesley 1974.

Slobodkin, Louis. The wide-awake owl. Macmillan 1958.

Wildsmith, Brian. The owl and the woodpecker. Watts 1971.

Freeman, Don. Fly high, fly low. Viking 1957.

Merrill, Jean. The travels of Marco. Knopf 1956.

BIRDS *Robin*

Flack, Marjorie. The restless robin. Houghton 1937.

Simon, Norma. Benjy's bird. Whitman 1965.

Varley, Dimitry. The whirly bird. Knopf 1961.

BIRDS *Swan*

Anderson, Hans Christian. The ugly duckling. Macmillan 1955.

Unwin, Nora. Sinbad the Cygnet. John Day 1970.

Baylor, Byrd.   Hawk, I'm your brother.   Scribner 1976.

Borack, Barbara.   Someone small,   Harper & Row 1969.   (Parakeet)

Brown, Margaret Wise.   Wheel on the chimney.   Lippincott 1954.
   (Stork)

Freeman, Don.   Come again, pelican.   Viking 1961.

Glasgow, Aline.   Honschi.   Parents' Mag. Pr. 1972. (Chickadee)

Politi, Leo.   Song of the swallows.   Scribner 1949.   (Swallow)

Rossetti, Christina Georgina.   What is pink? Macmillan 1971 (Flamingo)

Sterling, Dorothy.   Ellen's blue jays.   Doubleday n.d.

Tudor, Tasha.   Thistly B.   Oxford 1949 (Canary)

Wildsmith, Brian.   The owl and the woodpecker.   Watts 1971.

Wolkstein, Diane.   The cool ride in the sky.   Knopf 1973. (Buzzard)

BIRTHDAYS

Averill, Esther. Jenny's birthday book. Harper 1954.

Barrett, Judi. Benjamin's 365 birthdays. Atheneum 1974.

Clifton, Lucille. Don't you remember? Dutton 1973.

Clymer, Eleanor, Horatio's birthday. Atheneum 1976.

DeArmand, Frances Ullman. A very, very, special day. Parents Mag., 1963.

Flack, Marjorie. Ask Mr. Bear. Macmillan 1958.

Goodall, John S. Shrewbettina's birthday. Harcourt 1971.

Hoban, Russell. A birthday for Frances. Harper 1968.

Iwasaki, Chihiro. The birthday wish. McGraw 1974.

Keats, Ezra Jack. A letter to Amy. Harper 1968.

Lenski, Lois. Surprise for Davy. Walck 1947.

Lexau, Joan. Me day. Dial 1971.

Livingston, Myra Cohn. Happy birthday! Harcourt 1964.

Lobel, Anita. A birthday for a princess. Harper 1973.

Pearson, Susan. Monnie hates Lydia. Dial 1975.

Rosenbaum, Eileen. A different kind of birthday. Doubleday 1969.

Sandberg, Inger. Nicholas' favorite pet. Delacorte 1969.

Schatz, Letta. When will my birthday be? McGraw 1962.

Seuss, Dr. Happy birthday to you! Random 1959.

Uchida, Yoshiko. The birthday visitor. Scribner 1975.

Uchida, Yoshiko. Sumi's special happening. Scribner 1966.

Watson, Nancy D. Annie's spending spree. Viking 1957.

Watson, Nancy Dingman.   Tommy's mommy's fish.   Viking 1971.

Young, Miriam.   Miss Suzy's birthday.   Parents' Mag., 1974.

Zolotow, Charlotte.   Mr. Rabbit and the lovely present.   Harper & Row
    1962.

BLACK AMERICANS

Alexander, Martha. Bobo's dream. Dial 1970.

Bourne, Miriam. Raccoons are for loving. Random 1968.

Caines, Jeanette. Daddy. Harper 1977.

Clifton, Lucille. Don't you remember? Dutton 1973.

Clifton, Lucille. My brother fine with me. Holt 1975.

Clifton, Lucille. Three wishes. Viking 1974.

Freeman, Don. Corduroy. Viking 1968.

Gray, Genevieve. Send Wendell. Mc-Graw-Hill 1974.

Greenberg, Polly. Oh Lord, I wish I was a buzzard. Macmillan 1968.

Greenfield, Eloise. First pink light. Crowell 1976.

Greenfield, Eloise. Me and Neesie. Crowell 1975.

Hodges, Elizabeth Jamison. Free as a frog. Addison-Wesley 1969.

Keats, Ezra Jack. Goggles. Macmillan 1969.

Keats, Ezra Jack. Hi, cat! Macmillan 1970.

Keats, Ezra Jack. A letter to Amy. Harper & Row 1968.

Keats, Ezra Jack. Pet show! Macmillan 1972.

Keats, Ezra Jack. The snowy day. Viking 1962.

Kempner, Carol. Nicholas. Simon & Schuster 1968.

Lexau, Joan. Benjie. Dial 1964.

Lexau, Joan. Benjie on his own. Dial 1970.

McGovern, Ann. Black is beautiful. Scholastic 1969.

Madian, Jon. Beautiful junk. Little 1968.

Mannheim, Grete. The two friends. Knopf 1968.

Rosenbaum, Eileen. Ronnie. Parents' Mag. Pr., 1969.

Scott, Ann. Big cowboy western. Lothrop 1965.

Scott, Ann. Sam. McGraw-Hill 1967.

Steptoe, John. Stevie. Harper & Row 1969.

Steptoe, John. Uptown. Harper & Row 1970.

Thomas, Ianthe. Lordy, Aunt Hattie. Harper 1973.

Van Leeuwen, Jean. Timothy's flower. Random House 1967.

C

CHARACTER TRAITS *Cooperation*

Beskow, Elsa. Pelle's new suit. Harper 1929.

Burton, Virginia Lee. Maybelle, the cable car. Houghton 1952.

Galdone, Paul. The little red hen. Seabury 1973.

Lionni, Leo. Swimmy. Pantheon 1963.

CHARACTER TRAITS *Curiosity*

Brown, Margaret Wise. Three little animals. Harper 1956.

Rey, H. A. Curious George. Houghton 1941. (and other books in the
series)

CHARACTER TRAITS *Generosity*

Keats, Ezra Jack. Louie. Morrow 1975.

Lionni, Leo. Tico and the golden wings. Pantheon 1964.

CHARACTER TRAITS *Greediness*

Ginsburg, Mirra. Two greedy bears. Macmillan 1976.

Kuskin, Karla. What did you bring me? Harper 1973.

Leydenfrost, Robert. The snake that sneezed. Putnam 1970.

Oxenbury, Helen. Pig tale. Morrow 1973.

Peet, Bill. Kermit the hermit. Houghton 1965.

CHARACTER TRAITS *Helpfulness*

Adshead, Gladys. Brownies--hush! Walck 1938.

Adshead, Gladys. Brownies--they're moving. Walck 1970.

Duvoisin, Roger. Veronica's smile. Knopf 1964.

Klein, Leonore. Only one ant. Hastings 1971.

Kraus, Robert. Herman the helper. Dutton 1974.

CHARACTER TRAITS *Independence, Individuality*

Burn, Doris. Andrew Henry's meadow. Coward 1965.

DeRegniers, Beatrice Schenk. A little house of your own. Harcourt 1954.

Fox, Paula. Good Ethan. Bradbury 1973.

Green, Mary McBurney. Is it hard? Is it easy? Young Scott Bks., 1960.

Hayes, Geoffrey. Bear by himself. Harper 1976.

Kraus, Robert. Owliver. Windmill 1974.

Lexau, Joan. Benjie on his own. Dial 1970.

Lionni, Leo. Tico and the golden wings. Pantheon 1964.

Pinkwater, Daniel Manus. The big orange splot. Hastings House 1977.

Sendak, Maurice. Pierre. Harper 1962.

Ungerer, Tomi. No kiss for mother. Harper 1973.

CHARACTER TRAITS *Meanness*

Lobel, Arnold. Prince Bertram the bad. Harper 1963.

Skorpen, Liesel Moak. That mean man. Harper 1968.

Udry, Janice. The mean mouse and other mean stories. Harper 1962.

CHARACTER TRAITS *Shyness*

Krasilovsky, Phyllis.　The shy little girl.　Houghton 1970.

Lexau, Joan.　Benjie.　Dial 1964.

Skorpen, Liesel.　Plenty for three.　Coward 1971.

CIRCUS

Allen, Jeffrey. Bonzini! The tattoed man. Little 1976.

Anno, Mitsumasa. Dr. Anno's magical midnight circus. Weatherhill 1972.

Ardizzone, Edward. Paul, the hero of the fire. Walck 1963.

Carroll, Ruth. The chimp and the clown. Walck 1968.

DeRegniers, Betrice Schenk. Circus. Viking 1966.

Freeman, Don. Bearymore. Viking 1976.

Huber, Ursula. The Nock family circus. Atheneum 1968.

Ipcar, Dahlov. The marvelous merry-go-round. Doubleday 1970.

Lent, Blaire. Pistachio. Little 1964.

Littell, Robert. Left and right with lion and Ryan. Cowles 1969. o.p.

Munari, Bruno. The circus in the mist. World Pub., 1968.

Palazzo, Tony. Bianco and the new world. Viking 1957.

Peet, Bill. Ella. Houghton 1964.

Peet, Bill. Randy's dandy lions. Houghton 1964.

Peppe, Rodney. Circus numbers. Delacorte 1969.

Petersham, Maud. Circus baby. Macmillan 1950.

Schreiber, Georges. Bambino goes home. Viking 1959.

Schreiber, Georges. Bambino, the clown. Viking 1947.

Seuss, Dr. If I ran the circus. Random 1956.

Slobodkina, Esphyr. Pezzo the peddler and the circus elephant. Abelard-Schuman 1967.

Wiese, Kurt. Rabbit bros. circus; One night only. Viking 1963.

Wildsmith, Brian. Brian Wildsmith's circus. Watts 1970.

Will. Circus ruckus. Harcourt 1954.

CITY LIFE

Binzen, William. Miguel's mountain. Coward-McCann 1968.

Bourne, Miriam Anne. Emilio's summer day. Harper 1966.

Brenner, Barbara. Barto takes the subway. Knopf 1961.

Burton, Virginia Lee. Little house. Houghton 1942.

Colman, Hila. Peter's brownstone house. Morrow 1963.

Felt, Sue. Rosa-too-little. Doubleday 1950.

Gaeddert, Lou Ann. Noisy Nancy and Nick. Doubleday 1970.

Grossbart, Francine. A big city. Harper 1966.

Hader, Berta. Big city. Macmillan 1947.

Hader, Berta. Snow in the city. Macmillan 1963.

Hitte, Kathryn. What can you do without a place to play? Parents' Mag.
    Pr., 1971.

Keats, Ezra Jack. Dreams. Macmillan 1974.

Keith, Eros. A small lot. Bradbury 1968.

Kesselman, Wendy. Angelita. Hill & Wang 1970.

Lexau, Joan. Benjie on his own. Dial 1970.

McGinley, Phyllis L. All around the town. Lippincott 1948.

Madian, Jon. Beautiful junk. Little 1968.

Merrill, Jean. The travels of Marco. Knopf 1956.

Rosenbaum, Eileen. Ronnie. Parents' Mag. Pr., 1969.

Rukeyser, Muriel. I go out. Harper 1961.

Schick, Eleanor. 5A and 7B. Macmillan 1967.

Schick, Eleanor. City in the summer. Macmillan 1974.

Schick, Eleanor.   City in the   winter.   Macmillan 1973.

Tresselt, Alvin.   It's time now! Lothrop 1969.

Tresselt, Alvin.   Wake up, city! Lothrop 1957.

Van Leeuwen, Jean.   Timothy's flower.   Random 1967.

Wise, William.   The story of Mulberry Bend.   Dutton 1963.

CLOTHING

Bannon, Laura.   Red mittens.   Houghton 1946.

Beskow, Elsa.   Pelle's new suit.   Harper 1929.

Charlip, Remy.   Harlequin and the gift of many colors.   Parents' Mag.
Pr. 1973.

De Paola, Tomie.   Charlie needs a cloak.   Prentice-Hall 1973.
(clothes making)

Elwart, Joan P.   Right foot, wrong foot.   Steck-Vaughn 1968.

Hoberman, Mary Ann.   All my shoes come in twos.   Little 1957.

Holl, Adelaide. Mrs. McGarrity's peppermint sweater. Lothrop 1966. o. p.

Kay, Helen.   One mitten Lewis.   Lothrop 1954.

Keats, Ezra Jack.   Jennie's hat.   Harper 1966.

Kellogg, Steven.   The mystery of the missing red mitten.   Dial 1974.

Matsuno, Masako.   A pair of red clogs.   World 1960.

Nodset, Joan.   Who took the farmer's hat?   Harper 1963.

Shaw, Richard.   Who are you today?   Warne 1970.

Slobodkin, Florence.   Too many mittens.   Vanguard 1958.

Taback, Simms.   Joseph had a little overcoat.   Random 1977.

Ungerer, Tomi.   The hat.   Parents' Mag. Pr. 1970.

Weiss, Harvey.   My closet full of hats.   Abelard-Schuman 1962.

Zion, Gene.   No roses for Harry!   Harper 1968.

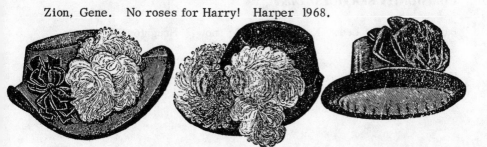

COMMUNITY SERVICES *Fire Department*

Gramatky, Hardie. Hercules. Putnam 1940.

Lenski, Lois. Little fire engine. Walck 1946.

Olds, Elizabeth. The big fire. Houghton 1945.

Quackenbush, Robert. There'll be a hot time in the old town tonight.
    Lippincott 1974.

COMMUNITY SERVICES *Library*

Felt, Sue. Rosa-too-little. Doubleday 1950.

Rockwell, Anne. I like the library. Dutton 1977.

Sauer, Julia Lina. Mike's house. Viking 1954.

COMMUNITY SERVICES *Police Department*

Lenski, Lois. Policeman Small. Walck 1962.

Schlein, Mariam. Amazing Mr. Pelgrew. Hale 1957.

COMMUNITY SERVICES *Other*

Burton, Virginia Lee. Katy and the big snow. Houghton 1943.
    (snowplow)

Zion, Gene. Dear garbage man. Harper 1957. (garbage removal)

COUNTRY LIFE

Brown, Margaret Wise.   Country noisy book.   Harper 1940.

Burton, Virginia Lee.   Little house.   Houghton 1942.

Coatsworth, Elizabeth.   The secret.   Macmillan 1965.

Dalgliesh, Alice.   The little wooden farmer.   Macmillan 1958.

Ipcar, Dahlov.   Brown cow farm.   Doubleday 1959.

Ipcar, Dahlov.   One horse farm.   Doubleday 1950.

Ipcar, Dahlov.   Ten big farms.   Knopf 1958.

Lenski, Lois.   The little farm.   Walck 1942.

Nakatani, Chiyoko.   My day on the farm.   Crowell 1976.

Provensen, Alice.   Our animal friends at Maple Hill Farm.   Random 1974.

Smith, Donald.   Farm numbers.   Abelard 1971.

Tresselt, Alvin.   Bonnie Bess the weathervane horse.   Parents' Mag. Pr., 1970.

Tresselt, Alvin.   Wake up, farm!   Lothrop 1955.

Tudor, Tasha.   The county fair.   Walck 1964.

Turkle, Brinton.   The adventures of Obadiah.   Viking 1972.

Watson, Nancy.   Katie's chickens.   Knopf 1965.

Watson, Nancy.   Sugar on snow.   Viking 1964.

Watson, Nancy.   What does A begin with?   Knopf 1956.

Wiberg, Harold.   Christmas at the Tomten's Farm.   Coward-McCann 1968.

d

DEATH

Bartoli, Jennifer. Nonna. Harvey House 1975.

Borack, Barbara. Someone small. Harper 1969.

Brown, Margaret Wise. The dead bird. Young Scott 1958.

Carrick, Carol. The accident. Seabury 1976.

Carrick, Carol. The foundling. Seabury 1977.

De Paola, Tomie. Nana upstairs and Nana downstairs. Putnam 1973.

Fassler, Joan. My grandpa died today. Behavioral Pub. 1971.

Kantrowitz, Mildred. When Violet died. Parents' Mag. Pr., 1973.

Viorst, Judith. The tenth good thing about Barney. Atheneum 1971.

Zolotow, Charlotte. My grandson Lew. Harper 1974.

EMOTIONS *Anger*

Du Bois, William Pene. The bear party. Viking 1951.

Hapgood, Miranda. Martha's mad day. Crown 1977.

Preston, Edna Mitchell. Temper tantrum book. Viking 1969.

Simon, Norma. I was so mad! Whitman 1974.

Zolotow, Charlotte. The quarreling book. Harper 1963.

EMOTIONS *Fear*

Babbitt, Natalie. The something. Farrar 1970.

Buckley, Helen E. Michael is brave. Lothrop 1971.

Greenberg, Barbara. The bravest babysitter. Dial 1977.

Heide, Florence Parry. Giants are very brave people. Parents' Mag. 1970.

Showers, Paul. A book of scary things. Doubleday 1977.

Skorpen, Liesel Moak. Michael. Harper 1975.

Williams, Gweniera. Timid Timothy. Scott 1944.

EMOTIONS *Other*

Holland, Ruth. A bad day. McKay 1964.

Pearson, Susan. Monnie hates Lydia. Dial 1975.

Sherman, Ivan. I do not like it when my friend comes to visit. Harcourt 1973 (jealousy)

Simon, Norma. I know what I like. Whitman 1971.

Viorst, Judith. Alexander and the terrible, horrible...day. Atheneum 1972.

Zolotow, Charlotte. The unfriendly book. Harper 1975.

FABLES, FAIRY TALES & FOLKLORE *Aesop*

Aesop.   Aesop's Fables.   Golden Press 1965.   o.p.

Aesop.   The hare and the tortoise; illus. by Paul Galdone.   McGraw 1962.

Duvoisin, Roger.   The miller, his son & their donkey.   McGraw 1962.

Kent, Jack.   More fables of Aesop.   Parents' Mag. Pr., 1974.

FABLES, FAIRY TALES & FOLKLORE *Africa*

Aardema, Verna.   Why mosquitoes buzz in people's ears.   Dial 1975.

Bernstein, Margery.   The first morning: an African myth.   Scribner 1976.

Berson, Harold.   Kassim's shoes.   Crown 1977. (Morocco)

Berson, Harold.   Why the jackal won't speak to the hedgehog.   Seabury 1969 (Tunisia)

Domanska, Janina.   The coconut thieves.   Scribner 1964.

Lexau, Joan.   The crocodile and hen.   Harper 1969.

McDermott, Gerald.   The magic tree.   Holt 1973.

Roche, A.K.   The clever turtle.   Prentice-Hall 1970.

Why the sun and moon live in the sky.   Houghton 1968.

FABLES, FAIRY TALES & FOLKLORE *Arabia*

Arabian Nights.   The flying carpet; illus. by Marcia Brown.   Scribner 1965.

Kirn, Ann.   Nine in a line.   Grosset n.d.

FABLES, FAIRY TALES & FOLKLORE *China*

Bishop, Claire. Five Chinese brothers. Hale 1938.

Holland, Janice. You never can tell. Scribner 1963.

Rockwell, Anne. Gift for a gift. Parents' Mag. Pr., 1974.

Tresselt, Alvin. The legend of the willow plate. Parents' Mag. Pr., 1968.

FABLES, FAIRY TALES & FOLKLORE *France*

Berson, Harold. Balarin's goat. Crown 1972.

Brown, Marcia. Stone soup. Scribner 1947.

Galdone, Paul. Puss in boots. Seabury 1976.

Miller, Warren. King Carlo of Capri. Harcourt 1958.

Perrault, Charles. Puss in boots. illus. by Marcia Brown. Scribner 1952.

Rockwell, Anne. The wolf who had a wonderful dream. Crowell 1973.

Wiesner, William. Green noses. Scholastic 1969.

FABLES, FAIRY TALES & FOLKLORE *Germany*

Anglund, Joan W. Nibble nibble mousekin: A tale of Hansel & Gretel. Harcourt 1962.

Gag, Wanda. Gone is gone. Coward 1933.

Galdone, Paul. The table, the donkey, and the stick. McGraw-Hill 1976.

Grimm Brothers. The Bremen town musicians. McGraw 1968.

Grimm Brothers. Hans in luck. Abelard-Schuman 1975.

Grimm Brothers. Hansel and Gretel. Scribner 1975.

Grimm Brothers.   Jorinda and Joringel.   Scribner 1968.

Grimm Brothers.   Little red riding hood.   Harcourt 1968.

Grimm Brothers.   The luck child.   Atheneum 1968.

Grimm Brothers.   Rapunzel.   Harcourt 1961.

Grimm Brothers.   Rumplestiltskin.   Harcourt 1967.

Grimm Brothers.   The seven ravens.   Harcourt 1963.

Grimm Brothers.   The shoemaker and the elves.   Scribner 1960.

Grimm Brothers.   The sleeping beauty.   Harcourt 1959.

Grimm Brothers.   Snow white; illus. by Trina Schart Hyman.   Little, Brown 1974.

Grimm Brothers.   Snow White and Rose Red.   Delacorte 1965.

Grimm Brothers.   Snow White and the seven dwarfs; illus. by Nancy Ekholm Burkert.   Farrar 1972.

Grimm Brothers.   Snow White and the seven dwarfs.   Farrar 1972.

Grimm Brothers.   The valiant little tailor.   Harvey House 1967.

Hyman, Trina Schart.   The sleeping beauty.   Little, Brown 1977.

Van Woerkom, Dorothy.   The queen who couldn't bake gingerbread.   Knopf; distrib. by Random 1975

Watts, Bernadette.   Mother Holly.   Nord Sud Verlag, Switzerland 1972.

FABLES, FAIRY TALES & FOLKLORE   *Great Britain*

Brown, Marcia.   Dick Whittington & his cat.   Scribner 1950.

Calhoun, Mary.   The goblin under the stairs.   Morrow 1968.

Cooney, Barbara.   Chanticleer and the fox.   Crowell n.d.

Davies, Anthea.   Sir Orfeo.   Bradbury 1973.

Galdone, Paul.   The little red hen.   Seabury 1973.

Jack and the beanstalk.   Written by Walter De La Mare, illus. by Joseph Low.   Knopf 1959.

Jacobs, Joseph.   Johnny-cake.   Viking 1972.

Mr. Miacca; an English folk tale.   Illus. by Evaline Ness.   Holt 1967.

Seuling, Barbara.   The teeny tiny woman.   Viking 1976.

Stern, Simon.   The Hobyahs.   Prentice-Hall 1977.

Tom Tit Tot.   Illus. by Evaline Ness.   Scribner 1965.

Wilkinson, Barry.   The diverting adventures of Tom Thumb.   Harcourt 1969.

Zemach, Harve.   Duffy and the devil.   Farrar 1973.

FABLES, FAIRY TALES & FOLKLORE   *Hungary*

Ambrus, Victor G.   The Sultan's bath.   Harcourt 1972.

Ambrus, Victor G.   Three poor tailors.   Harcourt 1966.

Ginsburg, Mirra.   Two greedy bears.   Macmillan 1976.

FABLES, FAIRY TALES & FOLKLORE   *India*

Brown, Marcia.   Once a mouse.   Scribner 1961.

Galdone, Paul.   The monkey and the crocodile.   Seabury 1969.

Quigley, Lillian.   The blind men and the elephant.   Scribner 1959.

Saxe, John.   The blind men and the elephant.   McGraw 1963.

Skurzynski, Gloria.   The magic pumpkin.   Scholastic 1971.

FABLES, FAIRY TALES & FOLKLORE   *Italy*

De Paola, Tomie.   Strega Nona.   Prentice-Hall 1975.

Zemach, Harve.   Awake and dreaming.   Farrar 1969.

Zemach, Harve.   Too much nose.   Holt 1967.

FABLES, FAIRY TALES & FOLKLORE   *Japan*

Hodge, Margaret.   The wave.   Houghton 1964.

Kijima, Hajime.   The little white hen.   Harcourt 1967.

Lifton, Betty J.   The dwarf pine tree.   Atheneum 1963.

McDermott, Gerald.   The stonecutter.   Viking 1975.

Matsuno, Masako.   Taro and the bamboo shoot.   Pantheon 1964.

Matsutani, Miyoko.   The crane maiden.   Parents' Mag. Pr.   1968.

Matsutani, Miyoko.   The fisherman under the sea.   Parents' Mag. Pr.
1969.

Titus, Eve.   The two stonecutters.   Doubleday 1967.

Yashima, Taro.   Seashore story.   Viking 1967.

FABLES, FAIRY TALES & FOLKLORE   *Jewish*

Hirsh, Marilyn.   The Rabbi and the twenty-nine witches.   Holiday
House 1976.

Suhl, Yuri.   Simon Boom gives a wedding.   Scholastic 1972.

Zemach, Margot.   It could always be worse.   Farrar 1976.

FABLES, FAIRY TALES & FOLKLORE   *Puerto Rico*

Belpre, Pura.   Dance of the animals.   Warne 1972.

Belpre, Pura.   Juan Bobo and the Queen's necklace.   Warne 1962.
o.p.

Belpre, Pura.   Perez & Martina.   Warne 1961.

FABLES, FAIRY TALES & FOLKLORE *Russia*

Brown, Marcia.   The neighbors.   Scribner 1967.

Domanska, Janina.   The turnip.   Macmillan 1972.

Robbins, Ruth.   Baboushka and the three kings.   Parnassus 1960.

Zakhoder, Boris.   Rosachok.   Lothrop 1970.

FABLES, FAIRY TALES & FOLKLORE *Scandinavia*

Asbjornsen, Peter. The three Billy goats gruff; illus. by Marcia
    Brown.   Harcourt 1957.

Galdone, Paul.   The three Billy Goats Gruff.   Seabury 1973.

Little Tuppen; an old tale.   Illus. by Paul Galdone. Seabury 1967.

Lobel, Anita.   The troll music.   Harper & Row 1966.

FABLES, FAIRY TALES & FOLKLORE *Turkey*

Walker, Barbara.   The mouse and the elephant.   Parents' Mag. Pr.
    1969.

Walker, Barbara.   New patches for old.   Parents' Mag. Pr. 1974.

FABLES, FAIRY TALES & FOLKLORE *Ukraine*

Bloch, Marie.   Ivanko & the dragon.   Atheneum 1969.

Tresselt, Alvin.   The mitten.   Lothrop 1964.

FABLES, FAIRY TALES & FOLKLORE *United States*

Chase, Richard.   Jack and the three sillies.   Houghton 1950.

Credle, Ellis.   Big Fraid, little Fraid.   Nelson 1964.

Le Grand.   Cap'n Dow and the hole in the doughnut.   Abingdon, n.d.

Le Grand.   Why cowboys sing in Texas.   Abingdon n.d.

Lent, Blair.   John Tabor's ride.   Little, Brown 1966.

Susie Mariar: an old folk rhyme.   Illus. by Lois Lenski.   Walck 1967.

Wolkstein, Diane.   The cool ride in the sky.   Knopf 1973.

FABLES, FAIRY TALES & FOLKLORE *Other*

Aliki.   Three gold pieces.   Pantheon 1967.   (Greece)

Aulaire, Ingri d'.   Don't count your chicks.   Doubleday 1943.

Belting, Natalia.   The sun is a golden earring.   Holt 1962.

Brooke, Leslie.   The golden goose book.   Warne 1905.

Brooke, Leslie.   The story of the three little pigs.   Warne 1905.   o.p.

Brooke, Leslie.   The three bears.   Warne n.d.   o.p.

Chicken-little.   Chicken Licken, retold by Kenneth McLeish.
   Bradbury 1974.

Domanska, Janina.   The best of the bargain.   Greenwillow 1977.
   (Poland)

Frasconi, Antonio.   The snow and the sun.   Harcourt 1961.   (Spain)

Gaoldone, Paul.   The frog prince.   McGraw 1974.

Galdone, Paul.   The three little pigs.   Seabury 1970.

Ginsburg, Mirra.   How the sun was brought back to the sky.
   Macmillan 1975.   (Slovenia)

Ginsburg, Mirra.   The strongest one of all.   Greenwillow 1977.

Hogrogian, Nonny.   The contest.   Greenwillow 1976.   (Armenia)

The house that Jack built.   Illus. by Paul Galdone.   McGraw 1961.

Le Cain, Errol.   The white cat.   Bradbury 1973.

Maestro, Giulio. Tortoise's tug of war. Bradbury 1971. (South America)

Merrill, Jean. High, wide and handsome. Addison-Wesley 1964. (Burma)

Nic Leodhas, Sorche. Always room for one more. Holt 1965. (Scotland)

Showalter, Jean B. The donkey ride. Doubleday n.d. (Alsace-Lorraine)

The three wishes. Illus. by Paul Galdone. McGraw 1961.

FABLES, FAIRY TALES *Modern*

Andersen, Hans C.   Emperor's new clothes. Houghton 1949.

Andersen, Hans C.   Little match girl. Houghton 1968.

Andersen, Hans C.   The steadfast tin soldier. Scribner 1953.

Andersen, Hans C.   Thumbelina. Scribner 1961.

Andersen, Hans C.   The ugly duckling. Scribner 1965.

Andersen, Hans C.   The woman with the eggs. Crown 1974.

Babbitt, Samuel.   The forty-ninth magician. Pantheon 1966.

Briggs, Raymond.   Jim and the beanstalk. Coward 1970.

Clymer, Eleanor.   Take tarts as tarts is passing. Dutton 1974.

De Paola, Tomie.   Helga's dowry: A troll love story. Harcourt 1977.

Dickens, Charles.   The magic fishbone. Vanguard 1953.

Elkin, Benjamin. Gillespie and the guards. Viking 1956.

Elkin, Benjamin.   The loudest noise in the world. Viking 1954.

Kipling, Rudyard.   How the rhinoceros got his skin. Walker 1974.

Kumin, Maxine.   The wizard's tears. McGraw 1975.

Levitin, Sonia.   A single speckled egg. Parnassus 1976.

Levitin, Sonia.   Who owns the moon? Parnassus 1973.

Lobel, Anita.   A birthday for a princess. Harper 1973.

Lobel, Arnold.   Giant John. Hale 1964.

Lobel, Anita.   The seamstress of Salzburg. Harper 1970.

McGovern, Ann.   Too much noise. Houghton 1967.

Massie, Diane Redfield.   Briar Rose and the golden eggs. Parents' Mag. Pr. 1973.

Merrill, Jean. Red riding. Pantheon 1968.

Reesink, Maryke. Peter and the twelve-headed dragon. Harcourt n.d.

Ringi, Kjell. The stranger. Random 1968.

Schaeffler, Ursula. The thief and the blue rose. Harcourt 1967.

Schlein, Miriam. The sun, the wind, the sea and the rain. Abelard-Schuman 1960.

Schneider, Nina. Hercules the gentle giant. Hawthron 1969.

Shapiro, Irwin. Twice upon a time. Scribner 1973.

Schecter, Ben. Conrad's castle. Harper 1967.

Steig, William. The amazing bone. Farrar 1976.

Steig, William. Caleb and Kate. Farrar 1977.

Steig, William. Roland the minstrel pig. Harper 1968.

Taylor, Mark. The bold fisherman. Golden gate 1967.

Thurber, James. Many moons. Harcourt 1943.

Ungerer, Tomi. The three robbers. Atheneum 1962.

Wahl, Jan. Cabbage moon. Holt 1965.

Wersba, Barbara. Do tigers ever bite kings? Atheneum 1970.

Wiesner, William. Tops. Viking 1969.

Will. The magic feather duster. Harcourt 1958.

Williams, Jay. Petronella. Parents' Mag. Pr. 1973.

Yolen, Jane. The girl who loved the wind. Crowell 1972.

Yolen, Jane H. The little spotted fish. Seabury 1975.

Zemach, Harve. The princess and froggie. Farrar 1975.

Zemach, Harve. The tricks of Master Dabble. Holt 1965.

FAMILY RELATIONS *General*

Aliki.   June seven. Macmillan 1972.

Blaine, Marge.   ` The terrible thing that happened at our house.
   Parents 1975

Burn, Doris.   Andrew Henry's meadow.   Coward 1965.

Charlip, Remy.   Hooray for me! Parents' Mag. Pr., 1975.

Fenton, Edward.   Fierce John.   Holt 1969.

Freeman, Don.   The night the lights went out.   Viking 1958. o.p.

Gray, Genevieve.   Send Wendell.   McGraw 1974.

Hoban, Russell.   The sorely trying day.   Harper 1964.

Kerr, Sue Felt.   Weezie goes to school.   Whitman 1969.

Mannheim, Grete.   The two friends.   Knopf 1968.

Rosenbaum, Eileen.   Ronnie.   Parents' Mag. Pr., 1969.

Scott, Ann H.   Big cowboy western.   Lothrop 1965.

Scott, Ann H.   Sam.   McGraw 1967.

Segal, Lore.   Tell me a Mitzi.   Farrar 1970.

Sonneborn, Ruth.   Seven in a bed.   Viking 1968.

Waber, Bernard.   Good-bye, funny dumpy-lumpy.   Houghton 1977.

FAMILY RELATIONS *Adoption*

Buck, Pearl.   Welcome child.   Day 1963. o.p.

Wasson, Valentina P.   The chosen baby.   Lippincott 1977.

FAMILY RELATIONS *Brothers and Sisters*

Amoss, Berthe.   Tom in the middle.   Harper 1968.

Borack, Barbara.   Someone small.   Harper 1969.

Clifton, Lucille.   My brother fine with me.   Holt 1975.

Hazen, Barbara.   Why couldn't I be an only kid like you, Wigger.
Atheneum 1975.

Hoban, Russell.   Harvey's hideout.   Parents' Mag. Pr., 1969.

Lasker, Joe.   He's my brother.   Whitman 1974.

Mallett, Anne.   Here comes tagalong.   Parents' Mag. Pr., 1971.

Pearson, Susan.   Monnie hates Lydia.   Dial 1975.

Wells, Rosemary.   Don't spill it again, James.   Dial 1977.

Wells, Rosemary.   Noisy Nora.   Dial 1973.   (middle child)

Zolotow, Charlotte.   Big sister and little sister.   Harper 1966.

Zolotow, Charlotte.   If it weren't for you.   Harper 1966.

Zolotow, Charlotte.   A rose, a bridge, and a wild black horse.
Harper 1964.

FAMILY RELATIONS *Divorce or Single-parent Family*

Caines, Jeannette.   Daddy.   Harper 1977.

Lexau, Joan.   Emily and the klunky baby and the next-door dog.
Dial 1972.

Lexau, Joan.   Me day.   Dial 1971.

Lisker, Sonia O.   Two special cards.   Harcourt 1976.

Zindel, Paul.   I love my mother.   Harper 1975.

Borack, Barbara.   Grandpa.   Harper 1967.

Buckley, Helen E.   Grandfather and I.   Lothrop 1959. o.p.

Buckley, Helen E.   Grandmother and I.   Lothrop 1961.

Buckley, Helen E.   Wonderful little boy.   Lothrop 1970.

De Paola, Tomie.   Nana upstairs and Nana downstairs.   Putnam 1973.

Gauch, Patricia L.   Grandpa and me.   Putnam 1972.

Goldman, Susan.   Grandma is somebody special.   Whitman 1976.

Lenski, Lois.   Debbie and her grandma.   Walck 1967.

Skorpen, Liesel Moak.   Mandy's grandmother.   Dial 1975.

Wahl, Jan.   The fisherman.   Norton 1969.

Williams, Barbara.   Kevin's grandma.   Dutton 1975.

Zolotow, Charlotte.   My grandson Lew.   Harper 1974.

FAMILY RELATIONS *Parents*

Brown, Margaret Wise.   The runaway bunny.   Harper 1942.

Carton, Lonnie C.   Daddies.   Random 1963.

Delton, Judy.   My mom hates me in January.   Whitman 1977.

Ehrlich, Amy.   Zeke Silver Moon.   Dial 1972.

Fisher, Aileen.   My mother and I.   Crowell 1967.

Lexau, Joan.   Every day a dragon.   Harper 1967.

Merriam, Eve.   Mommies at work.   Knopf 1961.

Mizumura, Kazue.   If I were a mother.   Crowell 1968.

Parsons, Ellen.   Rainy day together.   Harper 1971.

Penn, Ruth Bonn.   Mommies are for loving.   Putnam 1962.

Puner, Helen Walker.   Daddies; what they do all day.   Lothrop 1946.

Watson, Nancy Dingman.   Tommy's mommy's fish.   Viking 1971.

Williams, Barbara.   Someday, said Mitchell.   Dutton 1976.

Zolotow, Charlotte.   When I have a little girl.   Harper 1965.

FAMILY RELATIONS *Separation from Parent*

Greenfield, Eloise.   First pink light.   Crowell 1976.

Sharmat, Marjorie.   I want mama.   Harper 1974.   (parent in hospital)

FISH

Amoss, Berthe.   The marvelous catch of old Hannibal.   Parents' Mag.
   Pr. 1970.

Kinney, Jean.   What does the tide do?   Young Scott Books 1966.

Lionni, Leo.   Fish is fish.   Pantheon   1970.

Lionni, Leo.   Swimmy.   Pantheon 1963.

Shaw, Thelma.   Juano and the wonderful fresh fish.   Addison-Wesley
   1969.

Valens, Evans G.   Wingfin and Topple.   World 1962.

Wildsmith, Brian.   Fishes.   Watts 1968.

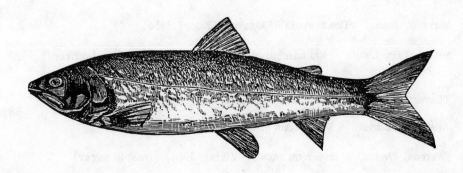

63

FOOD

Auerbach, Marjorie.   Seven uncles come to dinner.   Knopf 1963.

Barrett, Judi.   An apple a day.   Atheneum 1973.

Barrett, Judith.   Old MacDonald had an apartment house.   Atheneum 1969.

Brown, Marcia.   Stone soup.   Scribner 1947.

Devlin, Wende.   Cranberry Thanksgiving.   Parents' Mag. Pr., 1971.

Goffstein, M.B.   Fish for supper.   Dial 1976.

Hoban, Russell.   Bread and jam for Frances.   Harper 1964.

Janice.   Little bear learns to read the cookbook.   Lothrop 1969.

Janice.   Little bear's pancake party.   Lothrop 1960.

Kahl, Virginia.   The Duchess bakes a cake.   Scribner 1955.

Kahl, Virginia.   The perfect pancake.   Scribner 1960.

Kessler, Leonard.   Soup for the King.   Grosset 1969.

Le Grand.   Cap'n Dow and the hole in the doughnut.   Abingdon 1946.

McGowen, Tom.   Dragon stew.   Follett 1968. o.p.

Mahy, Margaret.   The witch in the cherry tree.   Parents' Mag. Pr. 1974.

Marshall, James.   Yummers! Houghton 1972.

Merrill, Jean.   The travels of Marco.   Knopf 1956.

Solot, Mary Lynn.   100 hamburgers; the getting thin book.   Lothrop 1972.

Thayer, Jane.   The blueberry pie elf.   Morrow 1961.

Watson, Aldren.   My garden grows.   Viking 1962.

Watson, Nancy.   Sugar on snow.   Viking 1964.   (maple sugar)

Zion, Gene.   The sugar mouse cake.   Scribner 1964.

FOR THE YOUNGER CHILD

Birnbaum, Abe.   Green eyes.   Golden Pr.,   1973.

Bright, Robert.   The friendly bear.   Doubleday 1971.

Bright, Robert.   Me and the bears.   Doubleday 1951.

Bright, Robert.   My hopping bunny.   Doubleday 1971.

Bright, Robert.   My red umbrella.   Morrow 1959.

Brown, Margaret Wise.   The golden egg book.   Western 1947.

Brown, Margaret Wise.   Goodnight moon.   Harper 1947.

Burningham, John.   The blanket.   Crowell 1976.

Burningham, John.   The cupboard.   Crowell 1976.

Burningham, John.   Mr. Gumpy's outing.   Holt 1970.

Carle, Eric.   The very hungry caterpillar.   Collins-World 1969.

Einsel, Walter.   Did you ever see?   Young Scott Bks.,   1962.

Ets, Marie H.   Elephant in a well.   Viking 1972.

Ets, Marie H.   Play we me.   Viking 1955.

Flack, Marjorie.   Ask Mr. Bear.   Macmillan 1958.

Ginsburg, Mirra.   The chick and the duckling.   Macmillan 1972.

Ginsburg, Mirra.   Mushroom in the rain.   Macmillan 1974.

Ginsburg, Mirra.   Three kittens.   Crown 1973.

Goffstein, M.B.   Fish for supper.   Dial 1976.

Hoban, Tana.   Where is it?   Macmillan 1974.

Hutchins, Pat.   Good-night, owl!   Macmillan 1972.

Hutchins, Pat.   Rosie's walk.   Macmillan 1968.

Hutchins, Pat.   Titch.   Macmillan 1971.

Iwasaki, Chihiro.   The birthday wish.   McGraw 1974.

Jensen, Virginia.   Sara and the door.   Addison-Wesley 1977.

Keats, Ezra Jack.   Kitten for a day.   Watts 1974.

Krauss, Ruth.   The bundle book.   Harper 1951.

Krauss, Ruth.   The happy day.   Harper 1949.

Lenski, Lois.   Davy goes places.   Walck 1961. (and other books by the author)

Matthiesen, Thomas.   Things to see; a child's world of familiar objects.   Platt & Munk 1966.

Nakatani, Chiyoko.   My day on the farm.   Crowell 1976.

Petersham, Maud.   The box with red wheels.   Macmillan 1973.

Rand, Ann.   I know a lot of things.   Harcourt 1956.

Rice, Eve.   Sam who never forgets.   Greenwillow 1977.

Rice, Eve.   What Sadie sang.   Greenwillow 1976.

Rockwell, Anne.   The toolbox.   Macmillan 1971.

Rockwell, Anne.   My doctor.   Macmillan 1973.

Rojankovsky, Feodor.   Animals on the farm.   Knopf 1967.

Skaar, Grace.   The very little dog and the smart little kitty.   Young Scott Bks., 1947.

Slobodkin, Louis.   The friendly animals.   Vanguard n.d.

Steiner, Charlotte.   My bunny feels soft.   Knopf 1958. o.p.

Williams, Garth.   The chicken book.   Delacorte 1970.

FRIENDSHIP

Anglund, Joan Walsh.   A friend is someone who likes you.   Harcourt 1958.

Binzen, William.   Carmen.   Coward-McCann 1969.

Brenner, Barbara.   Cunningham's rooster.   Parents' Mag. Pr., 1975.

Carlson, Natalie Savage.   Marie Louise and Christophe.   Scribner 1974.

Charlip, Remy.   Harlequin and the gift of many colors.   Parents' Mag. Pr., 1973.

Clifton, Lucille.   Three wishes.   Viking 1974.

Cohen, Miriam.   Best friends.   Macmillan 1971.

Cohen, Miriam.   Will I have a friend?   Macmillan 1967.

Ernst, Kathryn.   Owl's new cards.   Crown 1977.

Hoban, Russell.   Best friends for Frances.   Harper 1969.

Iwasaki, Chihiro.   Will you be my friend?   McGraw 1973.

Keats, Ezra Jack.   A letter to Amy.   Harper 1968.

Kennedy, Mary.   Come and see me.   Harper 1966.

Krasilovsky, Phyllis.   The shy little girl.   Houghton 1970.

Krasilovsky, Phyllis.   Susan sometimes.   Macmillan 1962.

Krauss, Ruth.   I'll be you and you be me.   Harper 1954.

Lionni, Leo.   Alexander and the wind-up mouse.   Pantheon 1969.

Lionni, Leo.   Little Blue and Little Yellow.   Obolensky 1959.

Mannheim, Grete.   The two friends.   Knopf 1968.

Marshall, James.   Willis.   Houghton 1974.

Rhodes, Dorothy.   Someone for Maria.   Golden Gate 1964.

Schick, Eleanor.   5A and 7B.   Macmillan 1967.

Schick, Eleanor.   Making friends.   Macmillan 1969.

Sherman, Ivan.   I do not like it when my friend comes to visit.
    Harcourt 1973.

Skorpen, Liesel.   Plenty for three.   Coward 1971.

Smaridge, Norah.   Peter's tent.   Viking 1965.

Udry, Janice May.   Let's be enemies.   Harper 1961.

Venable, Alan.   The checker players.   Lippincott 1973.

Vogel, Ilse-Margaret.   Hello Henry.   Parents' Mag. Pr., 1965.

Wilson, Christopher.   Hobnob.   Viking 1968.

Wright, Mildred.   A sky full of dragons.   Steck-Vaughn 1969.

Young, Miriam.   Can't you pretend?   Putnam 1970.

Zolotow, Charlotte.   The hating book.   Harper 1969.

Zolotow, Charlotte.   The new friend.   Abelard-Schuman 1968.

Zolotow, Charlotte.   The unfriendly book.   Harper 1975.

FROGS & TOADS

Flack, Marjorie.   Tim Tadpole and the great bullfrog.   Doubleday 1959.

Freschet, Berniece.   The old bullfrog.   Scribner 1972.

Galdone, Paul.   The frog prince.   McGraw 1974.

Keith, Eros.   Rrra-ah.   Bradbury 1969. (toad)

Kepes, Juliet.   Frogs merry.   Pantheon 1961.

Langstaff, John.   Frog went a-courtin.   Harcourt 1955.

Lionni, Leo.   Fish is fish.   Pantheon 1970.

Smith, Jim.   The frog band and the onion seller.   Little, Brown 1976.

Tresselt, Alvin.   Frog in the well.   Lothrop 1958.

Welber, Robert.   Frog, frog, frog.   Pantheon 1971.

Zemach, Harve.   The princess and froggie.   Farrar 1975.

g

GROWING PROBLEMS *Babysitter*

Chalmers, Mary.   Be good, Harry.   Harper & Row 1967.

Greenburg, Barbara.   The bravest babysitter.   Dial 1977.

Hughes, Shirley.   George the babysitter.   Prentice-Hall 1978.

GROWING PROBLEMS *Bedtime*

Cole, William.   Frances face-maker.   World 1963.

Crowe, Robert.   Clyde Monster.   Dutton 1976.

Hoban, Russell.   Bedtime for Frances.   Harper 1960.

Jewell, Nancy.   Calf, goodnight.   Harper 1973.

Johnson, La Verne.   Night noises.   Parents' Mag. Pr., 1968.

Johnston, Johanna.   Edie changes her mind.   Putnam 1964.

Leaf, Munro.   Boo, who used to be scared of the dark.   Random 1948.

Levine, Joan Goldman.   A bedtime story.   Dutton 1975.

Mayer, Mercer.   There's a nightmare in my closet.   Dial 1968.

Memling, Carl.   What's in the dark?   Parents' Mag. Pr.,   1971.

Plath, Sylvia.   The bed book.   Harper 1976.

Sharmat, Marjorie.   Goodnight, Andrew; Goodnight, Craig.   Harper 1969.

Slobodkin, Louis.   The wide-awake owl.   Macmillan 1958.

Viorst, Judith.   My mama says there aren't any zombies, ghosts, vampires, creatures, demons, monsters, fiends, goblins, or things.   Atheneum 1973.

Wells, Rosemary.   Miranda's pilgrims.   Bradbury 1970.

Zagone, Theresa.   No nap for me.   Dutton 1978.

GROWING PROBLEMS *Getting Lost*

Carrick, Carol.   The highest balloon on the common.   Greenwillow 1977.

Hader, Berta.   Lost in the zoo.   Macmillan 1951.

Kempner, Carol.   Nicholas.   Simon & Schuster 1968.

Lexau, Joan M.   Emily and the klunky baby and the next-door dog. Dial 1972.

Raskin, Ellen.   Moose, goose and little nobody.   Parents' Mag. Pr., 1974.

Sauer, Julia.   Mike's house.   Viking 1954.

Vogel, Ilse-Margaret.   Hello Henry.   Parents' Mag. Pr., 1965.

GROWING PROBLEMS *Hospital Experience*

Rey, Margaret.   Curious George goes to the hospital.   Houghton 1966.

Tamburine, Jean.   I think I will go the the hospital.   Abingdon 1965.

GROWING PROBLEMS *Imaginary Friend*

Greenfield, Eloise.   Me and Neesie.   Crowell 1975.

Hazen, Barbara S.   The gorilla did it.   Atheneum 1974.

Zolotow, Charlotte.   The three funny friends.   Harper 1961.

GROWING PROBLEMS *Losing Things*

Bannon, Laura.   Red mittens.   Houghton 1946.

Kay, Helen.   One mitten Lewis.   Lothrop 1954.

Kellogg, Steven.   The mystery of the missing red mitten.   Dial 1974.

Slobodkin, Florence.   Too many mittens.   Vanguard 1958.

GROWING PROBLEMS *Moving*

Brown, Myra Berry.   Pip moves away.   Golden Gate 1967. o.p.

Fisher, Aileen.   Best little house.   Crowell 1966.

Ilsley, Velma.   M is for moving.   Walck 1966.

Kantrowitz, Mildred.   Good-bye, kitchen.   Parents' Mag. Pr., 1972.

Marino, Dorothy.   Moving day.   Dial 1963. o.p.

Tobias, Tobi.   Moving day.   Knopf 1976.

Zolotow, Charlotte.   Janey.   Harper 1973.

GROWING PROBLEMS *New Experience*

Brown, Myra B.   First night away from home.   Watts 1960. o.p.

Buckley, Helen E.   Michael is brave.   Lothrop 1971.

Feagles, Anita.   The tooth fairy.   Young Scott Bks., 1962. (losing a tooth)

McCloskey, Robert.   One morning in Maine.   Viking 1952. (losing a tooth)

Raskin, Ellen.   Spectacles.   Atheneum 1968.

Schick, Eleanor.   Katie goes to camp.   Macmillan 1968.

Tresselt, Alvin.   The frog in the well.   Lothrop 1958.

Waber, Bernard.   Ira sleeps over.   Houghton 1972.

GROWING PROBLEMS *Running Away*

Alexander, Martha.   And my mean old mother will be sorry, blackboard bear.   Dial 1972.

Clifton, Lucille.   My brother fine with me.   Holt 1975.

Seligman, Dorothy Halle.   Run away home.   Golden Gate 1969.

GROWING PROBLEMS *Self*

Anglund, Joan Walsh.   Look out the window.   Harcourt 1959.

Charlip, Remy.   Hooray for me! Parents' Mag. Pr., 1975.

Domanska, Janina.   What do you see? Macmillan 1974.

Freeman, Don.   Dandelion.   Viking 1964.

Hodges, Elizabeth Jamison.   Free as a frog.   Addison-Wesley 1969.

Horvath, Betty.   Will the real Tommy Wilson please stand up.   Watts 1969.

Krasilovsky, Phyllis.   The shy little girl.   Houghton 1970.

Lionni, Leo.   Fish is fish.   Pantheon 1970.

Lionni, Loe.   Pezzettino.   Pantheon 1975.

Raskin, Ellen.   Moose, goose, and little nobody.   Parents' Mag. Pr., 1974.

Shaw, Richard.   Who are you today?   Warne 1970.

Supraner, Robyn.   Would you rather be a tiger?   Houghton 1973.

Wright, Dare.   Edith and Mr. Bear.   Random 1964.

GROWING PROBLEMS *Size*

Buckley, Helen E.   Wonderful little boy.   Lothrop 1970.

Hutchins, Pat.   Titch.   Macmillan 1971.

Krasilovsky, Phyllis.   The very little boy.   Doubleday 1962.

Krasilovsky, Phyllis.   The very little girl.   Doubleday 1953.

Krasilovsky, Phyllis. The very tall little girl. Doubleday 1969.

Krauss, Ruth. The growing story. Harper 1947.

Mallett, Anne. Here comes tagalong. Parents' Mag. Pr., 1971.

Schlein, Miriam. Billy, the littlest one. Whitman 1966.

Will. Chaga. Harcourt 1955.

GROWING PROBLEMS *Other*

Brown, Myra Berry. Benjy's blanket. Watts 1962. (security blanket) o.p.

Burden, Shirley. I wonder why... Doubleday 1963. (prejudice) o.p.

Burningham, John. The blanket. Crowell 1976. (security blanket)

Cohen, Miriam. Tough Jim. Macmillan 1974 (Bully)

Elwart, Joan. Daisy tells. Steck-Vaughn 1966. (keeping secrets) o.p.

Gaeddert, LouAnn. Noisy Nancy Norris. Doubleday 1965. (noisiness)

Hoban, Russell. Dinner at Alberta's. Crowell 1975. (manners)

Hutchins, Pat. Don't forget the bacon! Greenwillow 1976. (forgetting)

Johnston, Johanna. Speak up, Edie! Putnam 1974. (talking too much)

Klimowicz, Barbara. The strawberry thumb. Abingdon 1968. (thumb-sucking)

Lund, Doris Herold. You ought to see Herbert's house. Watts 1973. (exaggeration)

McGovern, Ann. Scram, kid! Viking 1974. (being left out)

Miles, Miska. Chicken forgets. Little, Brown 1976. (forgetting)

Ness, Evaline. Sam, bangs & moonshine. Holt 1966. (lying)

Quin-Harkin, Janet. Peter Penny's dance. Dial 1976.

Rey, Margret.   Spotty.   Harper 1945. (prejudice)

Rockwell, Anne.   The awful mess.   Parents' Mag. Press 1973.
  (untidiness)

Sharmat, Marjorie.   I'm terrific.   Holiday House 1977. (vanity)

Sherman, Ivan.   I do not like it when my friend comes to visit.   Harcourt
  1973. (visitors)

Turkle, Brinton.   The adventures of Obadiah.   Viking 1972. (honesty)

Uchida, Yoshiko.   The birthday visitor.   Scribner 1975. (visitors)

Wells, Rosemary.   Benjamin & Tulip.   Dial 1973. (bully)

Wright, Dare.   Edith and Mr. Bear.   Random 1964. (lying)

h

HEALTH

Averill, Esther. Jenny's bedside book. Harper 1959.

Brown, Myra Berry. Casey's sore-throat day. Watts 1964. o.p.

Fassler, Joan. Howie helps himself. Whitman 1975. (child in wheel-chair)

Goodsell, Jane. Katie's magic glasses. Houghton 1965.

Lasker, Joe. He's my brother. Whitman 1974. (child with learning problem)

Lerner, Marguerite. Dear little mumps child. Lerner 1959.

Lerner, Marguerite. Michael gets the measles. Lerner 1959.

Lerner, Marguerite. Peter gets the chickenpox. Lerner 1959.

Raskin, Ellen. Spectacles. Atheneum 1968.

Rockwell, Harlow. My dentist. Greenwillow 1975.

Rockwell, Harlow. My doctor. Macmillam 1973.

Solot, Mary Lynn. 100 hamburgers; the getting thin book. Lothrop 1972.

Williams, Jay. Pettifur. Four winds 1977. (weight)

HISTORY

Cooney, Barbara.   A garland of games and other diversions.   Holt
1969. (American colonies)

The Erie Canal.   Illus. by Peter Spier.   Doubleday 1970.

Hopkinson, Francis.   The battle of the kegs.   Crowell 1964. (U.S.
Revolution)

Lawson, Robert.   They were strong and good.   Viking 1940.

Lobel, Arnold.   On the day Peter Stuyvesant sailed into town.   Harper
1971.

London Bridge is falling down! Illus. by Peter Spier.   Doubleday 1967.

Lowitz, Sadyebeth.   General George the Great.   Stein & Day 1960.

Lowitz, Sadyebeth.   The magic fountain.   Stein & Day 1962. (Ponce
de Leon)

Lowitz, Sadyebeth.   The Pilgrims' party.   Stein & Day 1959.

Quackenbush, Robert.   There'll be a hot time in the old town tonight.
Lippincott 1974. (Chicago fire)

Schackburg, Richard.   Yankee Doodle.   Prentice-Hall 1965.

Schweitzer, Byrd Baylor.   One small blue bead.   Macmillan 1965.
(Prehistoric man)

Surany, Anico.   Malachy's gold.   Holiday 1968. (California gold rush)

Sweet Betsy from Pike.   Adapted and illus. by Roz Abisch and Bosche
Kaplan.   McCall 1970.

Waber, Bernard.   Just like Abraham Lincoln.   Houghton 1964.

Whittier, John G.   Barbara Frietchie.   Crowell n.d. (U.S. Civil War)

Wise, William.   The story of Mulberry Bend.   Dutton 1963.

HOLIDAYS *General*

Friedrich, Priscilla. The Easter bunny that overslept. Lothrop 1957.

Tudor, Tasha. A time to keep: the Tasha Tudor book of holidays. Rand McNally 1977.

Zolotow, Charlotte. Over and over. Harper 1957.

HOLIDAYS *Chinese New Year*

Handforth, Thomas. Mei Li. Doubleday 1938.

Politi, Leo. Moy Moy. Scribner 1960.

HOLIDAYS *Christmas*

Aichinger, Helga. The Shepherd. Crowell 1967.

Anglund, Joan Walsh. Christmas is a time of giving. Harcourt 1961.

Baker, Laura Nelson. The friendly beasts. Parnassus 1957.

Barry, Robert. Mr. Willowby's Christmas tree. McGraw 1963.

Belting, Natalia. Christmas folk. Holt 1969.

Briggs, Raymond. Father Christmas. Coward 1973.

Bright, Robert. Georgie's Christmas carol. Doubleday 1975.

Broun, Heywood C. A shepherd. Prentice-Hall 1967. o.p.

Brown, Margaret W. Christmas in the barn. Crowell 1952.

Brown, Margaret W. The little fir tree. Crowell 1954. o.p.

Brown, Margaret W. On Christmas eve. Young Scott Books 1961.

Brown, Margaret W. A pussycat's Christmas. Crowell 1949.

Brunhoff, Jean de.   Babar and Father Christmas.   Random 1949.

Budbill, David.   Christmas tree farm.   Macmillan 1974.

Carley, Wayne.   Charley the mouse finds Christmas.   Garrard 1972.

Chafetz, Henry.   The legend of Befana.   Houghton 1958.

Chalmers, Mary.   A Christmas story.   Harper 1956.

Clifton, Lucille.   Everett Anderson's Christmas coming.   Holt 1971.

Du Bois, William Pene.   Mother Goose for Christmas.   Viking 1973.

Duvoisin, Roger.   Christmas whale.   Knopf 1945.

Duvoisin, Roger.   One thousand Christmas beards.   Knopf 1955.

Duvoisin, Roger.   Petunia's Christmas.   Knopf 1952.

Ets, Marie Hall.   Nine days to Christmas.   Viking 1959.

Fenner, Carol.   Christmas tree on the mountain.   Harcourt 1966.

Francoise.   Noel for Jeanne-Marie.   Scribner 1953.

Gramatky, Hardie.   Happy's Christmas.   Putnam 1970.

Hoban, Russell.   Emmet Otter's jug-band Christmas.   Parents' Mag. Pr., 1971.

Hoban, Russell.   The mole family's Christmas.   Parents' Mag. Pr., 1969.

Hoffmann, Felix.   The story of Christmas.   Atheneum 1975.

Holmes, Efner Tudor.   The Christmas cat.   Crowell 1976.

Hoover, Helen.   Great wolf and the good woodsman.   Parents' Mag. Pr., 1967.

Hurd, Edith Thacher.   Christmas eve.   Harper 1962.

Janice.   Little Bear's Christmas.   Lothrop 1964.

Johnson, Crockett.   Harold at the North Pole.   Harper 1958.

Joslin, Sesyle. Baby elephant and the secret wishes. Harcourt 1962.

Juchen, Aurel von. The holy night. Atheneum 1968.

Keats, Ezra Jack. The little drummer boy. Macmillan 1968.

Konkle, Janet. The Christmas kitten. Childrens Pr., 1953.

Krahn, Fernando. How Santa Claus had a long and difficult journey delivering his presents. Delacorte 1970.

Kroeber, Theodora. A green Christmas. Parnassus 1967.

Lindgren, Astrid. Christmas in noisy village. Viking 1963.

Lindgren, Astrid. Christmas in the stable. Coward 1962.

McGinley, Phyllis. The year without a Santa Claus. Lippincott 1957.

Manifold, Laurie Fraser. The Christmas window. Houghton 1971.

Mariana. Miss Flora McFlimsey's Christmas eve. Lothrop 1949.

Monsell, Helen Albee. Paddy's Christmas. Knopf 1942.

Moore, Clement. The night before Christmas. Illus. by Gyo Fujikawa. Grosset & Dunlap 1961.

Moore, Clement. The night before Christmas. Illus. by Leonard Weisgard. Grosset & Dunlap 1949.

Moore, Clement. The night before Christmas. Illus. by Grandma Moses. Random 1948, 1961.

Peterson, Hans. Erik and the Christmas horse. Lothrop 1970.

Politi, Leo. Pedro, the angel of Olvera Street. Scribner 1946.

Robbins, Ruth. Baboushka and the three kings. Parnassus 1960.

Seuss, Dr. How the Grinch stole Christmas. Random 1957.

Thayer, Jane. Gus was a Christmas ghost. Morrow 1970.

Thirteen days of Yule. Illus. by Nonny Hogrogian. Crowell 1968.

Trent, Robbie. First Christmas. Harper 1948.

Tudor, Tasha. The doll's Christmas. Walck 1950.

Welch, Jean L. The animals came first. Walck 1963.

Wells, Rosemary. Morris's disappearing bag: a Christmas story.
Dial 1975.

Wiberg, Harold. Christmas at the Tomten's farm. Coward 1968.

Will. Christmas bunny. Harcourt 1953.

Wright, Dare. A gift from the lonely doll. Random 1966.

HOLIDAYS *Easter*

Adams, Adrienne. The Easter egg artists. Scribner 1976.

Armour, Richard. The adventure of Egbert the Easter egg. McGraw
1965.

Brown, Margaret W. The golden egg book. Golden Press 1947.

Duvoisin, Roger. Easter treat. Knopf 1954.

Friedrich, Priscilla. The Easter bunny that overslept. Lothrop 1957.

Heyward, Du Bose. Country bunny and the little gold shoes. Houghton
1939.

Kay, Helen. An egg is for wishing. Abelard-Schuman 1966. o.p.

Keats, Ezra Jack. Jennie's hat. Harper 1966.

Mariana. Miss Flora McFlimsey's Easter bonnet. Lothrop 1951.

Milhous, Katherine. The egg tree. Scribner 1950.

Tresselt, Alvin. The world in the candy egg. Lothrop 1967.

Tudor, Tasha. A tale for Easter. Walck 1941.

Zolotow, Charlotte. The bunny who found Easter. Parnassus
1959.

HOLIDAYS *Groundhog Day*

Cohen, Carol.   Wake up, groundhog.   Crown 1975.

Kesselman, Wendy.   Time for Jody.   Harper 1975.

Wiese, Kurt.   The groundhog and his shadow.   Viking 1959.

HOLIDAYS *Halloween*

Adams, Adrienne.   A woggle of witches.   Scribner 1971.

Balian, Lorna.   Humbug witch.   Abingdon 1965.

Barton, Byron.   Hester.   Greenwillow 1975.

Bright, Robert.   Georgie.   Doubleday 1959.   (and other books in the series)

Byfield, Barbara.   The haunted ghost.   Doubleday 1973.

Calhoun, Mary.   The witch of hissing hill.   Morrow 1964.

Calhoun, Mary.   Wobble the witch cat.   Morrow 1958.

Coombs, Patricia.   Dorrie and the Halloween plot.   Lothrop 1976. (and other books in the series)

Edmondson, Madeleine.   The witch's egg.   Seabury 1974.

Foster, Doris Van Liew.   Tell me Mr. Owl.   Lothrop 1957.

Freeman, Don.   Space witch.   Viking 1959.

Freeman, Don.   Tilly witch.   Viking 1969.

Hoff, Syd.   Mrs. Switch.   Putnam 1966.

Hurd, Edith Thacher.   The so-so cat.   Harper 1964.

Keith, Eros.   Bedita's bad day.   Bradbury 1971.

Mahy, Margaret.   The witch in the cherry tree.   Parents' Mag. Pr., 1974.

83

Mariana.   Miss Flora McFlimsey's Halloween.   Lothrop 1972.

Massey, Jeanne.   The littlest witch.   Knopf 1959.

Miller, Edna.   Mousekin's golden house.   Prentice-Hall 1964.

Preston, Edna Mitchell.   One dark night.   Viking 1969.

Sandberg, Inger.   Little ghost Godfrey.   Delacorte 1968.

Shire, Ellen.   The dancing witch.   McGraw-Hill 1965.

Slobodkin, Louis.   Trick or treat.   Macmillan 1959.

√Tudor, Tasha.   Pumpkin moonshine.   Walck 1938.

Varga, Judy.   Once-a-year witch.   Morrow 1973.

Young, Miriam.   The witch mobile.   Lothrop 1969.

Zolotow, Charlotte.   A tiger called Thomas.   Lothrop 1963.

HOLIDAYS *Hanukkah*

Chanover, Hyman.   Happy Hanukkah everybody.   United Synagogue
   Commission on Jewish Education 1969, c1954.

Coopersmith, Jerome.   A Chanukah fable for Christmas.   Putnam 1969.

HOLIDAYS *Passover*

Chanover, Hyman.   Pesah is coming! United Synagogue Commission on
   Jewish Education.

Chanover, Hyman.   Pesah is here! United Synagogue Commission on
   Jewish Education.

Shulevitz, Uri.   The magician.   Macmillan 1973.

HOLIDAYS *St. Patrick's Day*

√Calhoun, Mary.   The hungry leprechaun.   Morrow 1962.

Janice.   Little bear marches in the St. Patrick's Day parade.   Lothrop
     1967.

HOLIDAYS   *Thanksgiving*

Balian, Lorna.   Sometimes it's turkey - sometimes it's feathers.
     Abingdon 1973.

Child, Lydia Maria.   Over the river and through the wood.   Coward
     1974.

Devlin, Wende.   Cranberry Thanksgiving.   Parents' Mag. Pr.,   1971.

Janice.   Little bear's Thanksgiving.   Lothrop 1967.

Johnston, Johanna.   Speak up Edie!   Putnam 1974.   (child in Thanks-
     giving play)

Lowitz, Sadyebeth.   Pilgrims' party.   Dell 1977.

Zion, Gene.   The meanest squirrel I ever met.   Scribner 1962.

HOLIDAYS   *Valentine's Day*

Bulla, Clyde Robert.   The Valentine cat.   Crowell 1959.

Cohen, Miriam.   "Bee my Valentine".   Greenwillow 1978.

Mariana.   Miss Flora McFlimsey's Valentine.   Lothrop 1962.

HOLIDAYS   *Other*

Janice.   Little bear's New Year's party.   Lothrop 1973.

Mariana.   Miss Flora McFlimsey's May Day.   Lothrop 1969.

i

IMAGINATION

Alexander, Martha. Blackboard bear. Dial 1969.

Allen, Jeffrey. Bonzini! The tattooed man. Little 1976.

Arneson, D.J. Secret places. Holt 1971.

Burningham, John. Come away from the water, Shirley. Crowell 1977.

Carrick, Malcolm. Splodges. Viking 1976.

Charlip, Remy. Thirteen. Parents' Mag. Pr., 1975.

Fenton, Edward. Fierce John. Holt 1969.

Greenfield, Eloise. Me and Neesie. Crowell 1975.

Hazen, Barbara S. The gorilla did it. Atheneum 1974.

Hoban, Russell. Goodnight. Norton 1966.

Johnston, Johanna. Supposings. Holiday 1967.

Kellogg, Steven. Can I keep him? Dial 1971.

Kellogg, Steven. The mystery of the missing red mitten. Dial 1974.

Krauss, Ruth. I'll be you and you be me. Harper 1954.

Kravetz, Nathan. Is there a lion in the house? Walck 1970.

Lobel, Arnold. The man who took the indoors out. Harper 1974.

Lund, Doris Herold. Did you ever? Parents' Mag. Pr., 1965.

Lund, Doris Herold. You ought to see Herbert's house. Watts 1973.

McGovern, Ann. Scram, kid! Viking 1974.

McGovern, Ann. Zoo, where are you? Hale 1964.

Mayer, Marianna. Me and my flying machine. Parents' Mag. Pr., 1971.

Merrill, Jean. Red riding. Pantheon 1968.

Nolan, Dennis. Wizard McBean and his flying machine. Prentice-Hall 1977.

Rice, Inez. A long, long time. Lothrop 1964.

Schatz, Letta. A rhinocerous? preposterous! Steck-Vaughan 1965.

Scott, Ann. Big cowboy western. Lothrop 1965.

Selden, George. I see what I see! Ariel books 1962.

Sendak, Maurice. Maurice Sendak's really rosie starring the Nutshell Kids. Harper 1975.

Shaw, Richard. Who are you today? Warne 1970.

Shulevitz, Uri. One Monday morning. Scribner 1967.

Slobodkin, Louis. Magic Michael. Macmillan 1944.

Snyder, Zilpha Keatley. The princess and the giants. Atheneum 1973.

Stevenson, James. Could be worse. Greenwillow 1977.

Supraner, Robyn. Would you rather be a tiger? Houghton 1973.

Taylor, Mark. Henry explores the jungle. Atheneum 1968.

Taylor, Mark. Henry the explorer. Atheneum 1966.

Tobias, Tobi. A day off. Putnam 1973.

Wahl, Jan. Grandmother told me. Little 1972.

Wahl, Jan. A wolf of my own. Macmillan 1969.

Warner, Sunny. Tobias and his big red satchel. Knopf 1961.

Weiss, Harvey. My closet full of hats. Abelard-Schuman 1962.

Williams, Barbara. Someday, said Mitchell. Dutton 1976.

Young, Miriam.   Can't you pretend? Putnam 1970.

Young, Miriam.   Jellybeans for breakfast.   Parents' Mag., 1968.

Zimelman, Nathan.   Beneath the Oak tree.   Steck-Vaughn 1966.

Zimelman, Nathan.   Walls are to be walked. Dutton 1977.

Zolotow, Charlotte.   A rose, a bridge, and a wild black horse.   Harper
    1964.

Zolotow, Charlotte.   Someday. Harper 1965.

Zolotow, Charlotte.   When I have a little girl. Harper 1965.

INDIANS OF NORTH AMERICA

Baylor, Byrd. Hawk, I'm your brother. Scribner 1976.

Beatty, Hetty Burlingame. Little Owl Indian. Houghton 1951.

Blood, Charles. The goat in the rug. Parents' Mag. Pr., 1976.

Clark, Ann Nolan. In my mother's house. Viking 1941.

Goble, Paul. The friendly wolf. Bradbury 1975.

McDermott, Gerald. Arrow to the sun. Viking 1974.

Parish, Peggy. Good hunting, little Indian. Young Scott Bks., 1962.

Parish, Peggy. Snapping turtle's all wrong day. Simon & Schuster 1970.

Parnall, Peter. The great fish. Doubleday 1973.

Perrine, Mary. Salt Boy. Houghton 1968.

Russell, Solveig Paulson. Indian big and Indian little. Bobbs 1964.

Udry, Janice May. The sunflower garden. Harvey House 1969.

INSECTS *General*

Conklin, Gladys P.   We like bugs.   Holiday 1962.

Dugan, William.   The bug book.   Western 1977.

Kepes, Juliet.   Lady bird quickly.   Little 1964.

Lubell, Winifred.   The tall grass zoo.   Rand McNally 1960.

Petie, Harris.   Billions of bugs.   Prentice-Hall 1975.

INSECTS *Butterfly, Caterpillar*

Carle, Eric.   The very hungry caterpillar.   Collins-World 1969.

Conklin, Gladys P.   I like butterflies.   Holiday House 1960.

Conklin, Gladys P.   I like caterpillars.   Holiday 1958.

Goudey, Alice E.   Butterfly time.   Scribner 1964.

Politi, Leo.   The butterflies come.   Scribner 1957.

INSECTS *Cricket*

Caudill, Rebecca.   A pocketful of cricket.   Holt 1964.

Reid, Barbara.   Carlo's cricket.   McGraw 1967.

INSECTS *Other*

Aardema, Verna.   Why mosquitoes buzz in peoples ears.   Dial 1975.

Brandenberg, Franz.   Fresh cider and pie.   Macmillan 1973.

Portal, Colette.   The life of a Queen.   Braziller 1964.

Waber, Bernard.   A firefly named Torchy.   Houghton 1970.

INVERTEBRATES

Brandenberg, Franz. Fresh cider and pie. Macmillan 1973. (spider)

Freschet, Berniece. The web in the grass. Scribner 1972. (spider)

Graham, Margaret Bloy. Be nice to spiders. Harper 1967.

Lionni, Leo. The biggest house in the world. Pantheon 1968. (snail)

Lionni, Leo. Inch by inch. Obolensky 1960, 1962. (worm)

Peet, Bill. Kermit the hermit. Houghton 1965. (crab)

Ungerer, Tomi. Emile. Harper 1960. (octopus)

Waber, Bernard. I was all thumbs. Houghton 1975. (octopus)

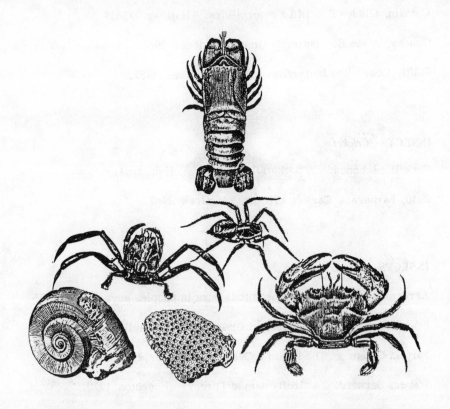

m

MALE/FEMALE ROLES

Blaine, Marge. The terrible thing that happened at our house. Parents' Mag. Pr., 1975.

Gaeddert, Lou Ann. Noisy Nancy and Nick. Doubleday 1970.

Haas, Irene. The Maggie B. Atheneum 1975.

Isadora, Rachel. Max. Macmillan 1976.

Klein, Norma. Girls can be anything. Dutton 1973.

Merriam, Eve. Mommies at work. Knopf 1961.

Rockwell, Harlow. My doctor. Macmillan 1973.

Rockwell, Harlow. My nursery school. Greenwillow 1976.

Schlein, Miriam. The girl who would rather climb trees. Harcourt 1975.

Tompert, Ann. Little fox goes to the end of the world. Crown 1976.

Van Woerkom, Dorothy. The queen who couldn't bake gingerbread. Knopf; distrib. by Random 1975.

Williams, Jay. Petronella. Parents' Mag. Pr., 1973.

Young, Miriam. Jellybeans for breakfast. Parents' Mag. Pr., 1968.

Zolotow, Charlotte. William's doll. Harper & Row 1972.

MATHEMATICS

Alain. 1, 2, 3, Going to the sea; an adding and subtracting book. Scholastic 1969.

Allen, Robert. Numbers. Platt & Munk 1968.

Bishop, Claire. Twenty-two bears. Viking 1964.

Blegvad, Lenore. One is for the sun. Harcourt 1968.

Carle, Eric. 1, 2, 3 to the zoo. World 1968.

Carle, Eric. The very hungry caterpillar. Collins-World 1969.

Duvoisin, Roger. Two lonely ducks. Knopf 1955.

Eichenberg, Fritz. Dancing in the moon. Harcourt 1956.

Feelings, Muriel L. Mojo means one. Dial 1971.

. Fisher, Margery M. One and one. Dial 1963.

Francoise. Jeanne-Marie counts her sheep. Scribner 1957.

Friskey, Margaret. Chicken Little count-to-ten. Childrens' Press 1946.

Gretz, Susanna. Teddy bears 1 to 10. Follet 1969.

Hoban, Tana. Count and see. Macmillan 1972.

Ipcar, Dahlov. Brown cow farm. Doubleday 1959.

Johnson, Crockett. Harold and the purple crayon. Harper 1958.

Kruss, James. 3 x 3: Three by three. Macmillan 1965.

Langstaff, John. Over in the meadow. Harcourt 1957.

McLeod, Emile Warren. One snail and me. Little 1961.

Mack, Stan. 10 bears in my bed. Pantheon 1974.

Martin, Patricia Miles. That cat! 1-2-3. Putnam 1969.

Peppe, Rodney. Circus numbers. Delacorte 1969.

Petie, Harris.   Billions of bugs.   Prentice-Hall 1975.

Reiss, John J.   Numbers.   Bradbury 1971.

Sendak, Maurice.   One was Johnny.   Harper 1962.

Sesame Street book of numbers.   NAL 1971.

Tudor, Tasha.   1 is one.   Walck 1956.

Vogel, Ilse-Margaret.   1 is no fun but 20 is plenty!   Hale 1965.

Wildsmith, Brian.   Brian Wildsmith's 1, 2, 3's.   Watts 1965.

Williams, Garth.   The chicken book.   Delacorte 1970.

Ziner, Feenie.   Counting carnival.   Coward 1962.

Zolotow, Charlotte.   One step, two...   Lothrop 1955.

MONSTERS

Aulaire, Ingri d'. The terrible troll-bird. Doubleday 1976.

Bloch, Marie Halun. Ivanko and the dragon. Atheneum 1969.

Bradfield, Roger. A good knight for dragons. Young Scott Bks., 1967.

Byfield, Barbara. The haunted ghost. Doubleday 1973.

Crowe, Robert. Clyde monster. Dutton 1976.

Flora, James. The great green turkey creek monster. Atheneum 1976.

Galdone, Joanna. The tailypo: a ghost story. Seabury Press 1977.

Hamada, Hirosuke. The tears of the dragon. Parents' Mag. Pr., 1967.

Holl, Adelaide. Sir Kevin of Devon. Lothrop 1963.

Kellogg, Steven. The mysterious tadpole. Dial 1977.

Kent, Jack. There's no such thing as a dragon. Golden Press 1975.

Lord, Beman. A monster's visit. Walck 1967. o.p.

McGowen, Tom. Dragon stew. Follett 1968. o.p.

Mayer, Mercer. Mrs. Beggs & the wizard. Parents' Mag. Pr., 1973.

Mayer, Mercer. Terrible troll. Dial 1968.

Mayer, Mercer. There's a nightmare in my closet. Dial 1968.

Peet, Bill. Cyrus the unsinkable sea serpent. Houghton 1975.

Riley, James Whitcomb. The gobble-uns'll git you ef you don't watch out! Lippincott 1975.

Sendak, Maurice. Where the wild things are. Harper 1963.

Stern, Simon. The Hobyahs. Prentice-Hall 1977.

Trez, Denise. Little knight's dragon. World 1963.

Ungerer, Tomi. The beast of Monsieur Racine. Farrar 1971.

Ungerer, Tomi.   Zeralda's ogre.   Harper 1967.

Viorst, Judith.   My mama says there aren't any zombies, ghosts,
    vampires, creatures, demons, monsters, fiends, goblins, or
    things.   Atheneum 1973.

Williams, Jay.   Everyone knows what a dragon looks like.   Four Winds
    1976.

Yolen, Jane H.   The little spotted fish.   Seabury 1975.

n

NATURE STUDY

Bancroft, Henrietta. Down come the leaves. Crowell 1961.

Bason, Lillian. Castles and mirrors and cities of sand. Lothrop 1968.

Bemelmans, Ludwig. Parsley. Harper 1955. (wildflowers)

Berenstain, Stan & Jan. The Berenstain bears' science fair. Random 1977.

Blough, Glenn. After the sun goes down; the story of animals at night. McGraw 1961.

Brown, Margaret W. Nibble, nibble, poems for children. Young Scott Bks., n.d.

Budbill, David. Christmas tree farm. Macmillan 1974.

Carle, Eric. The tiny seed. Crowell 1970.

Carrick, Carol. The old barn. Bobbs 1966.

Carrick, Carol. Swamp spring. Macmillan 1969.

Collier, Ethel. Who goes there in my garden? Young Scott Bks., 1963.

Conklin, Gladys. I caught a lizard. Holiday 1967.

Conklin, Gladys. I like butterflies. Holiday 1960.

Conklin, Gladys. If I were a bird. Holiday 1965.

Conklin, Gladys. I like caterpillars. Holiday 1958.

Conklin, Gladys. We like bugs. Holiday 1962.

DePaola, Tomie. The quicksand book. Holiday House 1977.

Ernst, Kathryn. Mr. Tamarin's trees. Crown 1976. (ecology)

Fisher, Aileen. Best little house. Crowell 1966.

Fisher, Aileen.   Going barefoot.   Crowell 1960.

Fisher, Aileen.   In the middle of the night.   Crowell 1965.

Fisher, Aileen.   Listen, rabbit.   Crowell 1964.

Fisher, Aileen.   My mother and I.   Crowell 1967.

Fisher, Aileen.   Up, up the mountain.   Crowell 1968.

Fisher, Aileen.   We went looking.   Crowell 1968.

Freschet, Berniece.   The old bullfrog.   Scribner 1972.

Freschet, Berniece.   Turtle pond.   Scribner 1971.

Freschet, Berniece.   The web in the grass.   Scribner 1972. (spider)

Garelick, May.   Look at the moon.   Young Scott Bks., 1969.

George, Jean Craighead.   All upon a stone.   Crowell 1971.

Goudey, Alice E.   Butterfly time.   Scribner 1964.

Goudey, Alice E.   The day we saw the sun come up.   Scribner 1961.

Goudey, Alice E.   Houses from the sea.   Scribner 1959. (shells)

Green, Mary McBurney.   Everybody eats.   Young Scott Bks., 1961.

Green, Mary McBurney.   Everybody has a house.   Young Scott Bks., 1961.

Hawkinson, Lucy.   Birds in the sky.   Childrens Press 1965.

House, Charles.   The lonesome egg.   Norton 1968.

Howell, Ruth Rea.   Everything changes.   Atheneum 1968.

Kinney, Jean.   What does the tide do?   Young Scott Books 1966.

Lubell, Winifred.   The tall grass zoo.   Rand McNally 1960.

MacDonald, Golden.   The little island.   Doubleday 1946.

Mizumura, Kazue.   If I built a village.   Crowell 1971. (ecology)

Oppenheim, Joanne. Have you seen trees? Young Scott Bks., 1967.

Parnall, Peter. The great fish. Doubleday 1973. (ecology)

Parnall, Peter. The mountain. Doubleday 1971. (ecology)

Provensen, Alice. Who's in the egg? Golden Press 1970.

Rockwell, Anne. Head to toe. Doubleday 1973.

Russell, Solveig Paulson. All kinds of legs. Bobbs 1963.

Schlein, Miriam. The rabbit's world. Four Winds 1973.

Schoenherr, John. The barn. Little 1968.

Schwartz, Julius. The earth is your spaceship. McGraw 1963.

Selsam, Millicent. All kinds of babies. Four Winds 1967.

Selsam, Millicent. How to be a nature detective. Harper 1963.

Seuss, Dr. The Lorax. Random 1971. (ecology)

Shulevitz, Uri. Dawn. Farrar 1974.

Simon, Mina. Is anyone here? Atheneum 1967.

Tresselt, Alvin. The dead tree. Parents' Mag. Pr., 1972.

Tresselt, Alvin. Rain drop splash. Lothrop 1946.

Tresselt, Alvin. Under the trees and through the grass. Lothrop 1962.

Udry, Janice May. A tree is nice. Harper 1956.

Valens, Evan G. Wildfire. World 1964. (forest fire)

Walters, Marguerite. Small pond. Dutton 1966.

Zolotow, Charlotte. When the wind stops. Harper 1975.

p

PETS

Alexander, Martha.   No ducks in our bathtub.   Dial 1973.

Gackenbach, Dick.   Do you love me?   Seabury 1975.

Carrick, Carol.   The foundling.   Seabury 1977.

Conklin, Gladys.   I caught a lizard.   Holiday 1967.

Holl, Adelaide.   One kitten for Kim.   Addison-Wesley 1969.

Iwasaki, Chihiro.   What's fun without a friend?   McGraw 1975.

Keats, Ezra Jack.   Pet show!   Macmillan 1972.

Kellogg, Steven.   Can I keep him?   Dial 1971.

Kellogg, Steven.   My mysterious tadpole.   Dial 1977.

Martin, Patricia.   The rice bowl pet.   Crowell 1962.

Provensen, Alice.   My little hen.   Random 1973.

Reid, Barbara.   Miguel and his racehorse.   Morrow 1973.

Ross, G. Max.   When Lucy went away.   Dutton 1976.

Sandberg, Inger.   Nicholas' favorite pet.   Delacorte 1969.

Schatz, Letta.   A rhinocerous? preposterous!   Steck-Vaughan 1965.

Skorpen, Liesel M.   All the lassies.   Dial 1970.

Skorpen, Liesel M.   Michael.   Harper 1975. (rabbit)

Skorpen, Liesel M.   Old Arthur.   Harper 1972. (pet growing old)

Warren, Joyce.   A mouse to be free.   Seacliff 1973.

PHOTOGRAPHS

Arneson, D.J. Secret places. Holt 1971.

Binzen, Bill. Alfred goes house hunting. Doubleday 1974.

Binzen, Bill. Alfred the little bear. Doubleday 1970.

Binzen, Bill. Carmen. Coward 1970.

Binzen, Bill. First day in school. Doubleday 1972.

Binzen, Bill. Miguel's mountain. Coward 1968.

Brenner, Barbara. Barto takes the subway. Knopf 1961.

Brenner, Barbara. Faces. Dutton 1970.

De Regniers, Beatrice S. Circus. Viking 1966.

De Regniers, Beatrice S. The shadow book. Harcourt 1960.

Fox, Charles Philip. When spring comes. Reilly & Lee 1964.

Fox, Charles Philip. When summer comes. Reilly & Lee 1966.

Hoban, Tana. Circles, triangles and squares. Macmillan 1974.

Hoban, Tana. Count and see. Macmillan 1972.

Hoban, Tana. Dig, drill, dump, fill. Greenwillow 1975.

Hoban, Tana. Push pull, empty full. Macmillan 1972.

Hoban, Tana. Where is it? Macmillan 1974.

Holland, Viki. We are having a baby. Scribner 1972.

Howell, Ruth Rea. Everything changes. Atheneum 1968.

Humphrey, Henry. What is it for? Simon & Schuster 1969.

Hurd, Edith Thacher. Come with me to nursery school. Coward 1970.

Kesselman, Wendy. Angelita. Hill & Wang 1970.

Konkle, Janet. The Christmas kitten. Childrens Press 1953.

McGovern, Ann.   Black is beautiful.   Scholastic 1969.

Madian, Jon.   Beautiful junk.   Little 1968.

Mannheim, Grete.   The two friends.   Knopf 1968.

Matthiesen, Thomas.   ABC; an alphabet book.   Platt & Munk 1966.

Matthiesen, Thomas.   Things to see; a child's world of familiar
   objects.   Platt & Munk 1966.

Oppenheim, Joanne.   Have you seen roads?   Young Scott Bks., 1969.

Rosenbaum, Eileen.   A different kind of birthday.   Doubleday 1969.

Rosenbaum, Eileen.   Ronnie.   Parents' Mag. Pr., 1969.

Ruben, Patricia.   Apples to zippers.   Doubleday 1976.

Stewart, Elizabeth.   Kim the kitten.   Reilly & Lee 1961.

Welch, Martha.   Just like puppies.   Coward 1969.

Welch, Martha.   Pudding and pie.   Coward 1968.

Wright, Dare.   Lonely doll.   Doubleday 1957.   (and other books in
   the series)

Wright, Dare.   Look at a colt.   Random 1969.

Ylla.   The little elephant.   Harper 1956.   (and other books in the
   series)

PUERTO RICANS IN THE U.S.

Binzen, Bill. Carmen. Coward 1969.

Bourne, Miriam. Emilio's summer day. Harper 1966.

Brenner, Barbara. Barto takes the subway. Knopf 1961.

Keats, Ezra Jack. My dog is lost. Crowell 1960.

Kesselman, Wendy. Angelita. Hill & Wang 1970.

Sonneborn, Ruth. Friday night is papa night. Viking 1970.

Sonneborn, Ruth. Seven in a bed. Viking 1968.

r

RELIGIOUS STORIES

Bible, Old Testament.   Daniel. Shadrach, Mesach and Abednego.
  McGraw 1965. o.p.

Bible, Old Testament.   Ecclesiastes. Selections.   A time for all
  things.   Walck 1966.

Bible, Old Testament, Genesis.   The first seven days.   Crowell
  1962. o.p.

Bible, Old Testament, Psalms.   The Lord is my Shepherd.   Walck
  1965.

Bible, Selections.   Wings of the morning.   Walck 1968.

Curtis, Cecile.   He looks this way.   Warne 1965.

De Regniers, Beatrice.   David and Goliath.   Viking 1965.

Farber, Norma.   Where's Gomer.   Dutton 1974.

Field, Rachel Lyman.   Prayer for a child.   Macmillan 1973.

Francoise.   The thank-you book.   Scribner 1947.

Lenski, Lois.   Mr. and Mrs. Noah.   Crowell 1948.

Noah's Ark.   Illus. by Peter Spier.   Doubleday 1977.

One wide river to cross.   Adapted by Barbara Emberley.   Prentice-
  Hall 1966.

Petersham, Maude.   Christ child.   Doubleday 1931.

Rose, Elizabeth.   How St. Francis tamed the wolf.   Harcourt 1958.

Singer, Isaac Bashevis.   Why Noah chose the dove.   Farrar 1973.

Surany, Anico.   The burning mountain.   Holiday House 1965.

Webb, Clifford.   The story of Noah.   Warne   n.d.

Wiesner, William.   The tower of Babel.   Viking 1968.

Wynants, Miche.   Noah's Ark.   Harcourt 1965.

REPTILES *Alligator & Crocodile*

De Groat, Diane. Alligator's toothache. Crown 1977.

Hartelius, Margaret A. The chicken's child. Doubleday 1975.

Hoban, Russell. Dinner at Alberta's Crowell 1975.

Marshall, James. Willis. Houghton 1974.

Waber, Bernard. Lyle, Lyle, Crocodile. Houghton 1972. (and other books in the series)

Zakhoder, Boris. The crocodile's toothbrush. McGraw 1973.

REPTILES *Dinosaur*

Ipcar, Dahlov. The wonderful egg. Doubleday 1958.

Slobodkin, Louis. Dinny and Danny. Macmillan 1951.

Young, Miriam. If I rode a dinosaur. Lothrop 1974.

REPTILES *Snake & Lizard*

Carlson, Natalie Savage. Marie Louise and Christophe. Scribner 1974.

Conklin, Gladys P. I caught a lizard. Holiday 1967.

Leydenfrost, Robert. The snake that sneezed. Putnam 1970.

Ungerer, Tomi. Crictor. Harper 1958.

Wildsmith, Brian. Python's party. Watts 1974.

REPTILES *Turtle*

Freeman, Don. The turtle and the dove. Viking 1964.

Freschet, Berniece.   Turtle pond.   Scribner 1971.

Graham, Al.   Timothy turtle.   Viking 1949.

MacGregor, Ellen.   Theodore turtle.   McGraw 1955.

Marshall, James.   Yummers! Houghton 1972.

Roche, A.   The clever turtle.   Prentice-Hall 1969.

Wiese, Kurt.   The cunning turtle.   Viking 1956.

Williams, Barbara.   Albert's toothache.   Dutton 1974.

S

SCHOOL STORIES

Amoss, Berthe.   The very worst thing.   Parents' Mag. Pr., 1972.

Bemelmans, Ludwig.   Madeline.   Viking 1939.

Binzen, Bill.   First day in school.   Doubleday 1972.

Bourne, Miriam.   Raccoons are for loving.   Random 1968.

Caudill, Rebecca.   A pocketful of cricket.   Holt 1964.

Cohen, Miriam.   "Bee my Valentine".   Greenwillow 1978.

Cohen, Miriam.   Tough Jim.   Macmillan 1974.

Cohen, Miriam.   When will I read?   Greenwillow 1977.

Cohen, Miriam.   Will I have a friend?   Macmillan 1967.

Hurd, Edith Thacher.   Come with me to nursery school.   Coward 1970.

Isadora, Rachel.   Willaby.   Macmillan 1977.

Johnston, Johanna.   Speak up, Edie!   Putnam 1974. (school play)

Kantrowitz, Mildred.   Willy bear.   Parents' Mag. Pr., 1976.

Kerr, Sue.   Weezie goes to school.   Whitman 1969.

Lenski, Lois.   Debbie goes to nursery school.   Walck 1970.

Lenski, Lois. A dog came to school. Walck 1955.

Mannheim, Grete. The two friends. Knopf 1968.

Marino, Dorothy. Buzzy bear's first day at school. Watts 1970. o.p.

Rockwell, Harlow. My nursery school. Greenwillow 1976.

Schick, Eleanor. Little school at Cottonwood Corners. Hale 1965.

Surany, Anico. Monsieur Jolicoeur's umbrella. Putnam 1967.

Yashima, Taro. Crow boy. Viking 1955.

SEASHORE

Aldridge, Josephine Haskell.   A penny and a periwinkle.   Parnassus 1961.

Bason, Lillian.   Castles and mirrors and cities of sand.   Lothrop 1968.

Burningham, John.   Come away from the water, Shirley.   Crowell 1977.

Freeman, Don.   Come again, pelican.   Viking 1961.

Garelick, May.   Down to the beach.   Four Winds 1973.

Gauch, Patricia L.   Grandpa and me.   Putnam 1972.

Goudey, Alice E.   Houses from the sea.   Scribner 1959.

Iwasaki, Chihiro.   What's fun without a friend?   McGraw 1975.

Kinney, Jean.   What does the tide do?   Young Scott Bks., 1966.

Kumin, Maxine.   The beach before breakfast.   Putnam 1964.

Lionni, Leo.   On my beach there are many pebbles.   Obolensky 1961.

Loree, Kate.   Pails and snails.   Harvey House 1967.

McCloskey, Robert.   Time of wonder.   Viking 1957.

Ryder, Joanne.   A wet and sandy day.   Harper 1977.

Schick, Eleanor.   City in the summer.   Macmillan 1974.

Simon, Mina.   Is anyone here?   Atheneum 1967.

Sylvester, Natalie.   Summer on Cleo's island.   Farrar 1977.

Turkle, Brinton.   The sky dog.   Viking 1969.

Wright, Dare.   Holiday for Edith and the bears.   Doubleday 1958.

Zion, Gene.   Harry by the sea.   Harper 1965.

SEASONS *General*

Birnbaum, Abe. Green eyes. Golden Press 1973.

Carle, Eric. The tiny seed. Crowell 1970.

Collier, Ethel. Who goes there in my garden? Young Scott Bks., 1963.

Fisher, Aileen. I like weather. Crowell 1963.

Fisher, Aileen. Up, up the mountain. Crowell 1968.

Foster, Doris Van Liew. A pocketful of seasons. Lothrop 1960.

Howell, Ruth Rea. Everything changes. Atheneum 1968.

Ichikawa, Satomi. A child's book of seasons. Parents' Mag. Pr., 1975.

Jacobs, Leland B. Just around the corner. Holt 1964.

Kuskin, Karla. The bear who saw the spring. Harper 1961.

MacDonald, Golden. The little island. Doubleday 1946.

Schatz, Letta. When will my birthday be? McGraw 1962.

Sendak, Maurice. Chicken soup with rice. Harper 1962.

Surany, Anico. The covered bridge. Holiday 1967.

Tresselt, Alvin. It's time now! Lothrop 1969.

Tresselt, Alvin. Johnny Maple-leaf. Lothrop 1948.

Tudor, Tasha. Around the year. Walck 1957.

Tudor, Tasha. First delights. Hale 1966.

Tudor, Tasha. A time to keep: the Tasha Tudor book of holidays. Rand McNally 1977.

Udry, Janice May. A tree is nice. Harper 1956.

Vasiliu, Mircea. The year goes round. John Day 1964.

Victor, Joan Berg.   Sh-h! Listen again! Sounds of the seasons.   World 1969.

Walters, Marguerite.   Small pond.   Dutton 1966.

Zion, Gene.   The summer snowman.   Harper 1955.

Zolotow, Charlotte.   Summer is...   Abelard-Schuman 1967.

SEASONS *Autumn*

Bancroft, Henrietta.   Down come the leaves.   Crowell 1961.

Fisher, Aileen.   Where does everyone go?   Crowell 1961.

Lenski, Lois.   Now it's fall.   Walck 1948.

Marino, Dorothy.   Buzzy bear goes south.   Watts 1961.   o.p.

Marino, Dorothy.   Buzzy bear's busy day.   Watts 1965.   o.p.

Tresselt, Alvin.   Autumn harvest.   Lothrop 1951.

SEASONS *Spring*

Anglund, Joan Walsh.   Spring is a new beginning.   Harcourt 1963.

Carrick, Carol.   Swamp spring.   Macmillan 1969.

Fish, Helen Dean.   When the root children wake up.   Stokes n.d.

Fox, Charles Philip.   When spring comes.   Reilly & Lee 1964.

Francoise.   Springtime for Jeanne-Marie.   Scribner 1955.

Gay, Zhenya.   The nicest time of year.   Viking 1960.

Hurd, Edith Thacher.   The day the sun danced.   Harper 1965.

Kumin, Maxine.   Spring things.   Putnam 1961.

Lenski, Lois. Spring is here. Walck 1945.

Lewis, Richard. In a spring garden. Dial 1965.

Tresselt, Alvin. "Hi Mister Robin!" Lothrop 1950.

Zion, Gene. Really spring. Harper 1956.

SEASONS *Summer*

Bourne, Miriam Anne. Emilio's summer day. Harper 1966.

Fox, Charles Philip. When summer comes. Reilly & Lee 1966.

Kumin, Maxine. The beach before breakfast. Putnam 1964.

Lenski, Lois. On a summer day. Walck 1953.

Miles, Betty. A day of summer. Knopf 1962.

Scheer, Julian. Rain makes applesauce. Holiday 1964.

Schick, Eleanor. City in the summer. Macmillan 1974.

Schick, Eleanor. Katie goes to camp. Macmillan 1968.

Sylvester, Natalie. Summer on Cleo's island. Farrar 1977.

Thomas, Ianthe. Lordy, Aunt Hattie. Harper 1973.

Tresselt, Alvin. Sun up. Lothrop 1949.

Zolotow, Charlotte. The summer night. Harper 1974.

SEASONS *Winter*

Brown, Margaret Wise. Winter noisy book. Scott 1947.

Craft, Ruth. The winter bear. Atheneum 1975.

Fenner, Carol. Christmas tree on the mountain. Harcourt 1966.

Holl, Adelaide. The runaway giant. Lothrop 1967.

116

Kellogg, Steven. The mystery of the missing red mitten. Dial 1974.

Lenski, Lois. I like winter. Walck 1950.

Miles, Betty. A day of winter. Knopf 1961.

Sandburg, Helga. Joel and the wild goose. Dial 1963.

Schick, Eleanor. City in the winter. Macmillan 1973.

Slobodkin, Florence. Too many mittens. Vanguard 1958.

Tresselt, Alvin. White snow, bright snow. Lothrop 1947.

Welber, Robert. The winter picnic. Pantheon 1970.

SKILLS *Color*

Borten, Helen.   Do you see what I see?   Abelard 1959.

Duvoisin, Roger.   The house of four seasons.   Lothrop 1956.

Emberley, Ed.   Green says go.   Little 1968.

Hirsh, Marilyn.   How the world got its color.   Crown 1972.

Hoffman, Beth.   Red is for apples.   Random 1966.

Lionni, Leo.   Little blue and little yellow.   Astor-Honor 1959.

Lobel, Arnold.   The great blueness and other predicaments.   Harper 1968.

O'Neill, Mary.   Hailstones and halibut bones.   Doubleday 1961.

Purdy, Susan.   If you have a yellow lion.   Lippincott 1966.

Reiss, John.   Colors.   Bradbury 1969.

Rossetti, Christina.   What is pink?   Macmillan 1971.

Steiner, Charlotte.   My slippers are red.   Knopf 1957.

Wolff, Robert J.   Hello, yellow.   Scribner 1968.

SKILLS *Getting Dressed*

Elwart, Joan Potter.   Right foot, wrong foot.   Steck-Vaughn co., 1968. o.p.

Hoberman, Mary Ann.   All my shoes come in twos.   Little 1957.

Krauss, Ruth.   The backward day.   Harper 1950.

SKILLS *Language Arts*

Auerbach, Marjorie.   Seven uncles come to dinner.   Knopf 1963.

Brown, Marcia. Peter Piper's Alphabet. Scribner 1959.

Carle, Eric. All about Arthur. Watts 1974.

Cohen, Miriam. When will I read? Greenwillow 1977.

Ets, Marie Hall. Talking without words. Viking 1968.

Feelings, Muriel. Jambo means hello. Dial 1974. (Swahili)

Feelings, Muriel. Mojo means one. Dial 1971. (Swahili)

Graham, John. A crowd of cows. Harcourt 1968. o.p.

Hann, Jacquie. That man is talking to his toes. Four winds 1976.

Hutchins, Pat. Don't forget the bacon! Greenwillow 1976.

Hutchins, Pat. The surprise party. Macmillan 1969.

Janice. Little bear leans to read the cookbook. Lothrop 1969.

Janice. Little bear's pancake party. Lothrop 1960.

Krauss, Ruth. A hole is to dig. Harper 1952.

Merriam, Eve. A gaggle of geese. Knopf 1960. (collective names for animals)

Merriam, Eve. Small fry. Knopf 1965. (names for young of animals) o.p.

Parish, Peggy. Amelia Bedelia. Harper 1963.

Potter, Charles. More tongue tanglers and a rigamarole world. 1964. o.p.

Potter, Charles. Tongue tanglers. World 1962. o.p.

Reid, Alastair. Ounce, dice, trice. Little, Brown 1958.

Rockwell, Anne. Head to toe. Doubleday 1973. (parts of body)

Scarry, Richard.   Richard Scarry's best word book ever.   Golden Press 1963.

Schoolfield, Lucille D.   Sounds the letters make.   Little 1940.

Wildsmith, Brian.   Brian Wildsmith's wild animals.   Watts 1967.

SKILLS *Learning to Write*

Felt, Sue.   Rosa-too-little.   Doubleday 1950.

Johnston, Johanna.   That's right, Edie.

Krauss, Ruth.   I write it.   Harper & Row 1970.

SKILLS *Problem Solving & Puzzles*

Anno, Mitsumasa.   Anno's alphabet.   Crowell 1975.

Anno, Mitsumasa.   Topsy-turvies.   Walker/Weatherhill 1970.

Cameron, Polly.   The 2 ton canary & other nonsense riddles.   Coward 1965.

Livermore, Elaine.   Find the cat.   Houghton 1973.

Myller, Rolf.   Rolling round.   Atheneum 1963.

Peppe, Rodney.   Odd one out.   Viking 1974.

Quackenbush, Robert.   Go tell Aunt Rhody.   Lippincott 1973.

The Sesame Street book of puzzlers.   NAL 1971.

Shaw, Charles G.   It looked like split milk.   Harper 1947.

Thorndike, Susan.   The electric radish and other jokes.   Doubleday 1973.

Ungerer, Tomi.   Snail, where are you?   Harper 1962.

Wildsmith, Brian.   Brian Wildsmith's puzzles.   Watts 1970.

Withers, Carl.   The wild ducks and the goose.   Holt 1968.   (a drawing story)

Zacharias, Thomas.   But where is the green parrot?   Delacorte 1968.

SKILLS   *Response Books*

A-hunting we will go (Folksong).   Oh, a-hunting we will go.   Illus. by
  John Langstaff.   Atheneum 1974.

Barberis, France.   Would you like a parrot?   Scroll Press 1967.

Bonne, Rose.   I know an old lady.   Rand 1961.   o.p.

Brown, Margaret Wise.   Country noisy book.   Harper 1940.

Charlip, Remy.   Mother mother I feel sick...   Parents' Mag. Pr.,
  1966.

Cole, William.   Frances face-maker.   World 1971.

Einsel, Walter.   Did you ever see?   Young Scott Bks. 1962.

Garten, Jan.   The alphabet tale.   Random 1964.

Gay, Zhenya.   What's your name.   Viking 1955.

Krauss, Ruth.   The bundle book.   Harper 1951.

Kuskin, Karla.   Roar and more.   Harper 1956.

Kuskin, Karla.   Which horse is William?   Harper 1969.

Lewis, Stephen.   Zoo city.   Greenwillow 1976.

Livermore, Elaine.   Find the cat.   Houghton 1973.

Macdonald, Golden.   Whistle for the train.   Doubleday 1956.   o.p.

Raskin, Ellen.   Who, said Sue, said Whoo?   Atheneum 1973.

Rockwell, Anne.   Head to toe.   Doubleday 1973.

Shaw, Charles G.   It looked like split milk.   Harper 1947.

Silverstein, Shel.   Uncle Shelby's a giraffe and a half.   Harper 1964.

Sivulich, Sandra.   I'm going on a bear hunt.   Dutton 1973.

Three jovial huntsmen. Illus. by Susan Jeffers. Bradbury 1973.

Ungeror, Tomi. One, two, where's my shoe? Harper 1964.

SKILLS *Senses*

Aliki. My five senses. Crowell 1969.

Borten, Helen. Do you know what I know? Abelard-Schuman 1970.

Brenner, Barbara. Faces. Dutton 1970.

Brown, Margaret W. The important book. Harper 1949.

DeRegniers, Beatrice S. The shadow book. Harcourt 1960.

Hoban, Tana. Look again! Macmillan 1971.

Humphrey, Henry. What is it for? Simon & Schuster 1969.

Steiner, Charlotte. My bunny feels soft. Knopf 1958. o.p.

Tudor, Tasha. First delights. Hale 1966.

Vasiliu, Mircea. The world is many things. Day 1967.

SKILLS *Shape & Size*

Borten, Helen. Do you see what I see? Abelard-Schuman 1959.

Brenner, Barbara. Mr. Tall & Mr. Small. Young Scott Books 1966.

Budney, Blossom. A kiss is round. Lothrop 1954.

Emberley, Ed. The wing on a flea. Little 1961.

Freeman, Mae. Finding out about shapes. McGraw 1969.

Hoban, Tana. Circles, triangles and squares. Macmillan 1974.

Kettlekamp, Larry. Spirals. Prentice-Hall 1964.

Lionni, Leo. Inch by inch. Astor-Honor 1962.

Myller, Rolf. How big is a foot? Atheneum 1962.

Reiss, John J. Shapes. Bradbury 1974.

Kohn, Bernice. One day it rained cats and dogs. Coward 1965.

Rey, Margaret. Billy's picture. Harper 1948.

Schlein, Miriam. Heavy is a hippopotamus. Scott 1954.

Schlein, Miriam. Shapes. Scott 1952.

The Sesame Street book of shapes. NAL 1971.

Ueno, Noriko. Elephant buttons. Harper 1973.

Wildsmith, Brian. Brian Wildsmith's 1. 2. 3's. Watts 1965.

SKILLS *Sound*

Borten, Helen. Do you hear what I hear? Abelard-Schuman 1960.

Brown, Margaret W. The noisy book. Harper 1939. (and other books
   in the series)

Brown, Margaret W. Shh...bang. Harper 1943.

Einsel, Walter. Did you ever see? Young Scott Bks., 1962.

Elkin, Benjamin. Loudest noise in the world. Viking 1954.

Johnson, La Verne. Night noises. Parents' Mag. Pr., 1968.

Kuskin, Karla. Roar and more. Harper 1956.

Rand, Ann. Listen, listen. Harcourt 1970.

Sicotte, Virginia. A riot of quiet. Holt 1969.

Spier, Peter. Crash! bang! boom! Doubleday 1972.

Spier, Peter. Gobble, growl, grunt. Doubleday 1971.

Teal, Val. The little woman wanted noise. Rand McNally 1967.

Victor, Joan Berg.   Sh-h! listen again!   World 1969.

Wolff, Janet.   Let's imagine sounds.   Dutton 1962.

SKILLS *Time*

Abisch, Roz.   Do you know what time it is?   Prentice-Hall 1968.

Behn, Harry.   All kinds of time.   Harcourt 1950.

Burton, Virginia Lee.   Little house.   Houghton 1942.

Colman, Hila.   Watch that watch.   Morrow 1962.

The days of the week; selections by Beman Lord.   Walck 1968.

Francoise.   What time is it, Jeanne-Marie?   Scribner 1963.

Hutchins, Pat.   Clocks and more clocks.   Macmillan 1970.

Mendoza, George.   The scarecrow clock.   Holt 1971.

Rockwell, Anne.   The good llama.   World 1968.

SKILLS *Other Concepts*

Borten, Helen.   Do you move as I do?   Abelard 1963.

Crews, Donald.   We read: A to Z.   Harper 1967. (various concepts)

Elwart, Joan.   Right foot, wrong foot.   Steck-Vaughn 1968. (left &
   right)

Green, Mary McBurney.   Is it hard? is it easy?   Young Scott Bks., 1960.

Hoban, Tana.   Over, under and through, and other spatial concepts.
   Macmillan 1973.

Hoban, Tana.   Push pull, empty full.   Macmillan 1972. (opposites)

Littell, Robert.   Left and right with lion and Ryan.   Cowles 1969.
   (left & right) o.p.

McNamara, Louise.   Henry's pennies.   Watts 1972. (money) o.p.

Spier, Peter. Fast-slow, high-low. Doubleday 1972. (opposites)

Watson, Nancy D.   Annie's spending spree. Viking 1957. (money) o.p.

SLEEP, DREAMS & LULLABY

Bright, Robert.   Me and the bears.   Doubleday 1951.

Brown, Margaret Wise.   A child's goodnight book.   Scott 1950.

Brown, Margaret W.   Goodnight moon.   Harper 1947.

Greenfield, Eloise.   Africa dream.   Day 1977.

Hush little baby.   Illus. by Margot Zemach.   Dutton 1976.

Jeffers, Susan.   All the pretty horses.   Macmillan 1974.

Johnson, La Verne.   Night noises.   Parents' Mag. Pr., 1968.

Johnston, Johanna.   Edie changes her mind.   Putnam 1964.

Keats, Ezra Jack.   Dreams.   Macmillan 1974.

Lippman, Peter.   New at the zoo.   Harper 1969.

Lund, Doris Herold.   Did you ever dream?   Parents' Mag. Pr., 1969.

Mack, Stan.   10 bears in my bed.   Pantheon 1974.

Rowand, Phyllis.   It is night.   Harper 1953.

Schlein, Miriam.   Here comes night.   Whitman 1957.

Schneider, Nina.   While Susie sleeps.   Addison-Wesley 1948.

Sendak, Maurice.   In the night kitchen.   Harper 1970.

Seuss, Dr.   Dr. Seuss's sleep book.   Random 1962.

Sleep, baby, sleep.   Atheneum 1967.   o.p.

Slobodkin, Louis.   The wide-awake owl.   Macmillan 1958.

Storm, Theodore.   Little John.   Farrar 1972.

Unterecker, John.   The dreaming zoo.   Walck 1965.

Warburg, Sandol.   Curl up small.   Houghton 1964.

Zolotow, Charlotte.   I have a horse of my own.   Abelard-Schuman 1964.

Zolotow, Charlotte. Sleepy book. Lothrop 1958.

Zolotow, Charlotte. The summer night. Harper 1974.

SOCIAL STUDIES *Occupations*

Francoise. What do you want to be? Scribner 1957.

Ipcar, Dahlov. I like animals. Knopf 1960.

Kraus, Robert. Owliver. Windmill 1974.

Lenski, Lois. Cowboy small. Walck 1949.

Lenski, Lois. The little farm. Walck 1942.

Lenski, Lois. Little fire engine. Walck 1946.

Lenski, Lois. The little train. Walck 1940.

Lenski, Lois. Policeman Small. Walck 1962.

Lenski, Lois. When I grow up. Walck 1960.

Merriam, Eve. Mommies at work. Knopf 1961.

Misch, Robert Jay. At daddy's office. Knopf 1946.

Olds, Elizabeth. The big fire. Houghton 1945.

Puner, Helen Walker. Daddies; what they do all day. Lothrop 1969.

Rockwell, Harlow. My dentist. Greenwillow 1975.

Rockwell, Harlow. My doctor. Macmillan 1973.

Scarry, Richard. Busy, busy world. Golden Pr., 1965.

Scarry, Richard. What do people do all day? Random 1968.

Sesame Street book of people and things. NAL 1971.

Titus, Eve. Mr. Shaw's shipshape shoeshop. Parents' Mag. Pr., 1970.

SOCIAL STUDIES *Safety*

Leaf, Munro. Safety can be fun. Lippincott 1961.

Lenski, Lois. Policeman Small. Walck 1962.

MacDonald, Golden. Red light, green light. Doubleday 1944.

McLeod, Emilie Warren. The bear's bicycle. Little, Brown 1975.

Smaridge, Norah. Watch out! Hale 1965.

SONGS

A-Hunting we will go (Folksong). Oh, a-hunting we will go. Illus. by John Langstaff. Atheneum 1974.

Baker, Laura Nelson. The friendly beasts. Parnassus 1957.

Bonne, Rose. I know an old lady. Rand McNally 1961. o.p.

Conover, Chris. Six little ducks. Crowell 1976.

The Erie Canal. Illus. by Peter Spier. Doubleday 1970.

The fox went out on a chilly night. Illus. by Peter Spier. Doubleday 1961.

The green grass grows all around. Illus. by Hilde Hoffman. Macmillan 1968.

Hopkinson, Francis. The battle of the kegs. Crowell 1964.

Hurrah, we're outward bound! Illus. by Peter Spier. Doubleday 1968.

Hush little baby. Illus. by Margot Zemach. Dutton 1976.

Keats, Ezra Jack. The little drummer boy. Macmillan 1968.

Langstaff, John. Frog went a-courtin. Harcourt 1955.

Langstaff, John. Ol' Dan Tucker. Harcourt 1963.

Langstaff, John. Over in the meadow. Harcourt 1957.

Langstaff, John. The swapping boy. Harcourt 1960.

Mack, Stan. 10 bears in my bed. Pantheon 1974.

Mills, Alan. The hungry goat. Rand McNally 1964. o.p.

Mommy, buy me a china doll. Illus. by Harve Zemach. Farrar 1966.

Nic Leodhas, Sorche. Always room for one more. Holt 1965.

One wide river to cross. Prentice-Hall 1966.

Quackenbush, Robert. Go tell Aunt Rhody. Lippincott 1973.

Quackenbush, Robert.   There'll be a hot time in the old town tonight.
     Lippincott 1974.

Rounds, Glen.   Casey Jones, the story of a brave engineer.   Golden
     gate 1968.

Sawyer, Ruth.   Journey cake, ho!   Viking 1953.

Schackburg, Richard.   Yankee doodle.   Prentice-Hall 1965.

Sendak, Maurice.   Maurice Sendak's really rosie, starring the Nut-
     shell Kids.   Harper 1975.

Song of the sour plum; and other Japanese children's songs.   Walker
     1968.

Sweet Betsy from Pike.   Adapted and Illus. by Roz Abisch and Boche
     Kaplan.   McCall 1970.

Taylor, Mark.   The bold fisherman.   Golden Gate   1967.

Varlay, Rene.   Lollipop songs.   Holt 1962.

Weil, Lisl.   The Sorcerer's Apprentice.   Little 1962.

SPECIAL INTERESTS *Ballet*

Gauch, Patricia Lee. Christina Katerina and the first annual grand ballet. Coward 1974.

Isadora, Rachel. Max. Macmillan 1976.

Shire, Ellen. The dancing witch. McGraw 1965.

SPECIAL INTERESTS *Fairs*

Carrick, Carol. The highest balloon on the common. Greenwillow 1977.

Tudor, Tasha. Corgiville fair. Crowell 1971.

Tudor, Tasha. The county fair. Walck 1964.

SPECIAL INTERESTS *Fishing*

Goffstein, M.B. Fish for supper. Dial 1976.

Watson, Nancy Dingman. Tommy's mommy's fish. Viking 1971.

SPECIAL INTERESTS *Gardening*

Collier, Ethel. Who goes there in my garden? Young Scott Bks., 1963.

Van Leeuwen, Jean. Timothy's flower. Random 1967.

Watson, Aldren. My garden grows. Viking 1962.

SPECIAL INTERESTS *Music*

Brenner, Barbara. Cunningham's rooster. Parents' Mag. Pr., 1975.

McCloskey, Robert. Lentil. Viking 1940.

Prokofieff, Serge. Peter and the wolf. Knopf 1940.

Slobodkina, Esphyr. Boris and his balalaika. Abelard-Schuman 1964.

SPECIAL INTERESTS *Painting & Drawing*

Carrick, Malcolm. Splodges. Viking 1976.

Rey, Margret. Billy's picture. Harper 1948.

Spilka, Arnold. Paint all kinds of pictures. Walck 1963.

SPECIAL INTERESTS *Picnic*

Goodall, John. The surpise picnic. Atheneum 1977.

Unnerstad, Edith. The ditch picnic. Norton 1964.

Welber, Robert. The winter picnic. Pantheon 1970.

SPECIAL INTERESTS *Other*

Blood, Charles. The goat in the rug. Parents' Mag. Pr., 1976. (weaving)

Carrick, Carol. Sleep out. Seabury 1973.

Emberley, Ed. The parade book. Little 1962 . o.p.

Kerr, Judith. When Willy went to the wedding. Parents' Mag. Pr., 1973.

Martin, Patricia Miles. Calvin and the Cub Scouts. Putnam 1964.

Peet, Bill. Cyrus the unsinkable sea serpent. Houghton 1975. (pirates)

Willard, Nancy. Simple pictures are best. Harcourt 1976. (photography)

SPORTS & GAMES

Freeman, Don. Ski pup. Viking 1963.

Hitte, Kathryn. What can you do without a place to play? Parents' Mag. Pr., 1971.

Hoban, Russell. How Tom beat Captain Najork and his hired sportsmen. Atheneum 1974.

Isadora, Rachel. Max. Macmillan 1976. (baseball)

Keith, Eros. A small lot. Bradbury 1968.

London Bridge is falling down! Illus. by Peter Spier. Doubleday 1967.

Merrill, Jean. Here I come - Ready or not. Whitman 1970. (hide-and-seek)

Ormondroyd, Edward. Broderick. Parnassus 1969. (surfing)

Rosenbaum, Eileen. A different kind of birthday. Doubleday 1969.

Sachs, Marilyn. Matt's mitt. Doubleday 1975.

Thayer, Ernest. Casey at the bat. Watts 1965.

Uchida, Yoshiko. Sumi's prize. Scribner 1964. (kites)

Venable, Alan. The checker players. Lippincott 1973.

Wiese, Kurt. Fish in the air. Viking 1948. (kites)

Wright, Mildred Whatley. A sky full of dragons. Steck-Vaughn 1969. (kites)

t

TALES OF FAR AWAY *Africa*

Feelings, Muriel. Jambo means hello. Dial 1974.

Feelings, Muriel. Mojo means one. Dial 1971.

Greenfield, Eloise. Africa dream. Day 1977.

Jupo, Frank. Atu, the silent one. Holiday 1967.

Musgrove, Margaret. Ashanti to Zulu: African traditions. Dial 1976.

Webb, Clifford. A jungle picnic. Warne 1953.

TALES OF FAR AWAY *Alaska*

Creekmore, Raymond. Lokoshi learns to hunt seals. Macmillan 1967.

Scott, Ann H. On mother's lap. McGraw 1972.

TALES OF FAR AWAY *China*

Creekmore, Raymond. Little Fu. Macmillan 1947.

Flack, Marjorie. Story about Ping. Viking 1933.

Handforth, Thomas. Mei Li. Doubleday 1938.

Wiese, Kurt. Fish in the air. Viking 1948.

Williams, Jay. Everyone knows what a dragon looks like. Four Winds 1976.

Yolen, Jane. The emperor and the kite. Collins-World 1967.

TALES OF FAR AWAY *France*

Auerbach, Marjorie. Seven uncles come to dinner. Knopf 1963.

Bemelmans, Ludwig. Madeline. Viking Press 1939. (and other books in the series)

Diska, Pat. Andy says...Bonjour! Vanguard 1954.

Francoise. Minou. Scribner 1962.

Francoise. Noel for Jeanne-Marie. Scribner 1953. (and other books in the series)

Lamorisse, Albert. The red balloon. Doubleday 1956.

Robbins, Ruth. The emperor and the drummer boy. Parnassus 1962.

TALES OF FAR AWAY *Germany*

Schaad, Hans. Gunpowder tower. Harcourt 1967.

Schaad, Hans. The Rhine pirates. Harcourt 1968.

TALES OF FAR AWAY *Great Britain*

Bemelmans, Ludwig. Madeline in London. Viking 1961.

Reeves, James. Titus in trouble. Walck 1960.

TALES OF FAR AWAY *Hungary*

Surancy, Anico. Kati and Kormos. Holiday 1966.

Varga, Judy. Janko's wish. Morrow 1969.

TALES OF FAR AWAY *India*

Price, Christine. The valiant chattee-maker. Warne 1965.

Trez, Denise. The royal hiccups. Viking 1965.

Slobodkin, Louis. Polka-dot goat. Macmillan 1964.

TALES OF FAR AWAY *Italy*

Brown, Marcia. Felice. Scribner 1958.

Politi, Leo. Little Leo. Scribner 1951.

Reid, Barbara. Carlo's cricket. McGraw 1967.

Slobodkin, Louis. Picco, the sad Italian pony. Vanguard 1961.

Titus, Eve. Anatole in Italy. McGraw 1973.

Weil, Lisl. Melissa's friend Fabrizzio. Macmillan 1967.

TALES OF FAR AWAY *Japan*

Glasgow, Aline. Honschi. Parents Mag. Pr., 1972.

Hamada, Hirosuke. The tears of the dragon. Parents' Mag. Pr., 1967.

Matsuno, Masako. A pair of red clogs. World 1960.

Uchida, Yoshiko. Rokubei and the thousand rice bowls. Scribner 1962.

Uchida, Yoshiko. Sumi's prize. Scribner 1964.

Uchida, Yoshiko. Sumi's special happening. Scribner n.d.

Yashima, Taro. Crow boy. Viking 1955.

Yashima, Taro & Mitsu. Plenty to watch. Viking 1954.

Yashima, Taro. Village tree. Viking 1953.

TALES OF FAR AWAY *Lapland*

Aulaire, Ingri d'. Children of the northlights. Viking 1962.

Borg, Inga. Parrak - the white reindeer. Warne 1959.

TALES OF FAR AWAY *Mexico*

Kirn, Ann. Two pesos for Catalina. Rand McNally 1962.

Schweitzer, Byrd B. Amigo. Macmillan 1963.

TALES OF FAR AWAY *Netherlands*

Green, Norma. The hole in the dike. Crowell 1974.

Krasilovsky, Phyllis. The cow who fell in the canal. Doubleday 1972.

Reesink, Maryke. The golden treasure. Harcourt 1968.

TALES OF FAR AWAY *Norway*

Aulaire, Ingri d'. Ola. Doubleday 1932.

Aulaire, Ingri d'. The terrible troll-bird. Doubleday 1976.

TALES OF FAR AWAY *Peru*

Eiseman, Alberta. Candido. Macmillan 1965.

Surany, Anico. Ride the cold wind. Putnam 1964.

TALES OF FAR AWAY *Portugal*

Balet, Jan. Joanjo. Delacorte 1967.

Weil, Lisl. Eyes so-o big. Houghton 1964.

TALES OF FAR AWAY *Siam*

Ayer, Jacqueline. Nu Dang and his kite. Harcourt 1972.

Ayer, Jacqueline. A wish for little sister. Harcourt 1960.

Northrup, Mili. The watch cat. Bobbs-Merrill 1968.

TALES OF FAR AWAY *Spain*

Leaf, Munro. The story of Ferdinand. Viking 1936.

Shaw, Thelma. Juano and the wonderful fish. Addison-Wesley 1969.

TALES OF FAR AWAY *Sweden*

Beskow, Elsa. Pelle's new suit. Harper 1929.

Lindgren, Astrid. Children of Noisy Village. Viking 1962. (and other books in the series)

Lindgren, Astrid. The Tomten. Coward 1961.

Lindgren, Astrid. The Tomten and the fox. Coward 1965.

Peterson, Hans. Erik and the Christmas horse. Lothrop 1970.

Wibert, Harald. Christmas at the tomten's farm. Coward 1968.

TALES OF FAR AWAY *Switzerland*

Chonz, Selina. A bell for Ursli. Walck 1953.

Weil, Lisl. The hopping knapsack. Macmillan 1970.

TALES OF FAR AWAY *Other*

Ayer, Jacqueline. A wish for little sister. Harcourt 1960. (Thailand)

Brown, Marcia. Henry, fisherman. Scribner 1949. (Virgin Islands)

Hauff, Wilhelm. The adventures of Little Mouk. Macmillan 1974. (turkey)

Holding, James. Mr. Moonlight and Omar. Morrow 1963. (Morocco)

Kay, Helen. An egg is for wishing. Abelard-Schuman 1966. (Ukraine) o.p.

Kotzwinkle, William. The supreme, superb, exalted and delightful, one and only magic building. Farrar 1973.

Leaf, Munro. Wee Gillis. Viking 1938. (Scotland)

Quin-Harkin, Janet. Peter Penny's dance. Dial 1976. (around the world)

Rose, Anne K. How does a czar eat potatoes? Lothrop 1973.

Slobodkina, Esphyr. Boris and his Balalaika. Abelard 1964. (Russia)

Surany, Anico. The burning mountain. Holiday 1965. (El Salvador)

Surany, Anico. The golden frog. Putnam 1963. (Panama)

Surany, Anico. Lora, Lorita. Putnam 1969. (Columbia)

Surany, Anico. Monsieur Jolicoeur's umbrella. Putnam 1967. (Haiti)

Thompson, Vivian L. Keola's Hawaiian donkey. Golden Gate 1966.

Tooze, Ruth. Our rice village in Cambodia. Viking Pr., 1963. (Cambodia)

Zimelman, Nathan. Pepito. Reilly & Lee 1967. (Chile)

TOYS

Binzen, Bill. Alfred goes house hunting. Doubleday 1974.

Binzen, Bill. Alfred the little bear. Doubleday 1970.

Bornstein, Ruth. Annabelle. Fitzhenry & Whiteside 1978.

Craft, Ruth. The winter bear. Atheneum 1974.

Flora, James. Sherwood walks home. Harcourt 1966.

Freeman, Don. Corduroy. Viking 1968.

Gretz, Susanna. Teddybears abc. Follett 1975.

Johnston, Johanna. Sugarplum. Knopf 1955.

Johnston, Johanna. Sugarplum and Snowball. Knopf 1968.

Kantrowitz, Mildred. Willy bear. Parents' Mag. Pr., 1976.

Keats, Ezra Jack. Louie. Morrow 1975. (puppets)

Lenski, Lois. Debbie and her dolls. Walck 1970.

Ormondroyd, Edward. Theodore. Parnassus 1966.

Ormondroyd, Edward. Theodore's rival. Parnassus 1971.

Sandburg, Carl. The wedding procession of the rag doll and the broom handle and who was in it. Harcourt 1967.

Scharen, Beatrix. Gilgin and Till. Atheneum 1969.

Simon, Norma. Elly the elephant. St. Martins 1962.

Skorpen, Liesel M. Elizabeth. Harper 1970.

Steger, H. Travelling to Tripiti. Harcourt 1967.

Steiner, Charlotte. Tomboy's doll. Lothrop 1969.

Tudor, Tasha. The doll's Christmas. Walck 1950.

Van Stockum, Hilda. Little old bear. Viking 1962.

Wahl, Jan.   The muffletumps: A story of four dolls.   Holt 1966.

Wright, Dare.   Lonely doll.   Doubleday 1957.   (and other books in
    the series)

Zolotow, Charlotte.   William's doll.   Harper 1972.

TRANSPORTATION & OTHER MACHINERY   *General*

Gaeddert, Lou Ann. Noisy Nancy and Nick. Doubleday 1970.

Lenski, Lois. Davy goes places. Walck 1961.

Scarry, Richard. Richard Scarry's cars & trucks & things that go.
  Golden Press 1974.

Scarry, Richard. Richard Scarry's hop aboard! Here we go! Golden
  Press 1972.

Schlein, Miriam. How do you travel? Abingdon 1954.

Wright, Ethel. Saturday walk. Scott 1954.

Zaffo, George J. Giant nursery book of things that go. Doubleday
  1959.

Zaffo, George J. The giant nursery book of things that work. Doubleday 1967.

Zaffo, George J. The giant nursery book of travel fun. Doubleday
  1965.

TRANSPORTATION & OTHER MACHINERY   *Airplanes*

Gramatky, Hardie. Loopy. Putnam 1941.

Lenski, Lois. The little airplane. Walck 1938.

Mayer, Marianna. Me and my flying machine. Parents' Mag. Pr.,
  1971.

Young, Miriam. If I flew a plane. Lothrop 1970.

TRANSPORTATION & OTHER MACHINERY   *Automobiles*

Alexander, Anne. ABC of cars and trucks. Doubleday 1971.

Lenski, Lois. The little auto. Walck 1934.

Peet, Bill. Jennifer and Josephine. Houghton 1967.

Sandberg, Inger. The boy with 100 cars. Delacoret 1967.

TRANSPORTATION & OTHER MACHINERY *Boats*

Ardizzone, Edward. Tim's friend Towser. Walck 1962.

Flack, Marjorie. Boats on the river. Viking 1946.

Graham, Margaret Bloy. Benjy's boat trip. Harper 1977.

Gramatky, Hardie. Little Toot. Putnam 1939. (and other books in
  the series)

Haas, Irene. The Maggie B. Atheneum 1975.

Hurrah, we're outward bound! Illus. by Peter Spier, Doubleday 1968.

Lenski, Lois. The little sail boat. Walck 1937.

Mendoza, George. The alphabet boat. McGraw 1972.

Stearns, Monroe. Eric's journey. Lippincott 1960.

TRANSPORTATION & OTHER MACHINERY *Buses*

Kessler, Ethel. Big red bus. Doubleday 1957.

Shuttlesworth, Dorothy Edwards. ABC of buses. Doubleday 1965.

TRANSPORTATION & OTHER MACHINERY *Fire Engines*

Gramatky, Hardie. Hercules. Putnam 1940.

Lenski, Lois. Little fire engine. Walck 1946.

Olds, Elizabeth. The big fire. Houghton 1945.

TRANSPORTATION & OTHER MACHINERY *Subway*

Brenner, Barbara. Barto takes the subway. Knopf 1961.

Kempner, Carol. Nicholas. Simon & Schuster 1968.

TRANSPORTATION & OTHER MACHINERY *Trains*

Brown, Margaret Wise. Two little trains. Addison-Wesley 1949.

Burton, Virginia Lee. Choo Choo. Houghton 1937.

Gramatky, Hardie. Homer and the circus train. Putnam 1957.

Kessler, Ethel. All aboard the train. Doubleday 1964.

Macdonald, Golden. Whistle for the train. Doubleday 1956. o.p.

Lenski, Lois. The little train. Walck 1940.

Piper, Watty. Little engine that could. Platt 1961.

Rounds, Glen. Casey Jones, the story of a brave engineer. Golden Gate 1968.

Woolley, Catherine. I like trains. Hale 1965.

TRANSPORTATION & OTHER MACHINERY *Trucks & Tractors*

Burton, Virginia Lee. Katy and the big snow. Houghton 1943. (snow-plow)

Burton, Virginia Lee. Mike Mulligan and his steam shovel. Houghton 1939.

Hoban, Tana. Dig, drill, dump, fill. Greenwillow Books 1975.

Young, Miriam. If I drove a tractor. Lothrop 1973.

Young, Miriam. If I drove a truck. Lothrop 1967.

TRANSPORTATION & OTHER MACHINERY *Other*

Allen, Jeffrey. Mary Alice, operator number 9. Little, Brown 1975. (telephone)

Bate, Norman. Who built the bridge? Scribner 1954.

Brown, Marcia. The little carousel. Scribner 1946.

Burton, Virginia Lee. Maybelle, the cable car. Houghton 1952.

Du Bois, William Pene. Lazy Tommy pumpkinhead. Harper 1966. (machinery)

Gramatky, Hardie. Sparky. Putnam 1952. (trolley car) o.p.

Krahn, Fernando. The family minus. Parents' Mag. Pr., 1977. (inventions)

Oppenheim, Joanne. Have you seen roads? Young Scott 1969.

Rockwell, Anne. The toolbox. Macmillan 1971. (tools)

Slobodkin, Louis. The late cuckoo. Vanguard 1962. (clock)

Steig, William. Farmer Palmer's wagon ride. Farrar 1974.

Swift, Hildegarde. Little red lighthouse and the great gray bridge. Harcourt 1942.

Titus, Eve. Anatole and the robot. McGraw 1960.

Watts, Mabel. While the horses galloped to London. Parents' Mag. Pr., 1973. (stagecoach)

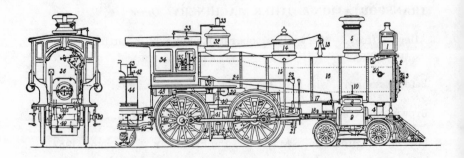

V

VERSE *General*

Anglund, Joan W. Morning is a little child. Harcourt 1969.

Brown, Margaret Wise. Nibble, nibble. Addison-Wesley 1959.

Clifton, Lucille. Everett Anderson's Christmas coming. Holt 1971.

Fisher, Aileen. Do bears have mothers too? Crowell 1973.

Fisher, Aileen. We went looking. Crowell 1968.

Greenaway, Kate. Marigold garden. Warne n.d.

Greenaway, Kate. Under the window. Warne 1900.

Hoffman, Hilde. The mountain bounder. Macmillan 1967.

Jacobs, Leland B. Alphabet of girls. Holt 1969.

Jacobs, Leland B. Just around the corner. Holt 1964.

Lewis, Richard. In a spring garden. Dial 1965. (haiku)

Mizumura, Kazue. I see the winds. Crowell 1966. (haiku)

O'Neill, Mary. Hailstones and halibut bones. Doubleday 1961.

Prelutsky, Jack. A gopher in the garden. Macmillan 1967.

Riley, James Whitcomb. The gobble-uns'll git you ef you don't watch
  out! Lippincott 1975.

Song of the sour plum; and other Japanese children's songs. Walker
  1968.

Spilka, Arnold. A lion I can do without. Walck 1964.

Stearns, Monroe. Underneath my apple tree. Lippincott 1960.

Stevenson, Robert Louis. A child's garden of verses. Golden Press
  1951.

Tagore, Rabindranath.   Moon, for what do you wait?   Atheneum 1967.

Thayer, Ernest.   Casey at the bat.   Watts 1965.

Wells, Rosemary.   Don't spill it again, James.   Dial 1977.

Whittier, John G.   Barbara Frietchie.   Crowell n.d.

VERSE   *Nonsense Verse*

Cameron, Polly.   "I can't" said the ant.   Coward 1961.

Charlip, Remy.   Mother mother I feel sick...   Parents' Mag. Pr., 1966.

De Regniers, Beatrice S.   Was it a good trade?   Harcourt 1956.

Lear, Edward.   The owl and the pussycat.   Little, Brown 1961.

Lear, Edward.   Whizz! Macmillan 1973.

Nolan, Dennis.   Wizard McBean and his flying machine.   Prentice-Hall 1977.

Preston, Edna Mitchell.   Pop corn & ma goodness.   Viking 1969.

Raskin, Ellen.   Who, said Sue, said whoo?   Atheneum 1973.

Silverstein, Shel.   Uncle Shelby's a giraffe and a half.   Harper 1964.

Spilka, Arnold.   A lion I can do without.   Walck 1964.

VERSE   *NurseryRhymes*

Anglund, Joan Walsh.   In a pumpkin shell.   Harcourt 1960.

Becker, John.   Seven little rabbits.   Walker 1973.

Bodecker, N.M., trans.   It's raining, said John Twaining.   Atheneum 1973.

Brooke, Leslie.   Johnny Crow's garden.   Warne 1903.

Caldecott, Randolph.   The babes in the woods.   Warne n.d.

Caldecott, Randolph. Come lasses and lads. Warne n.d.

Caldecott, Randolph. The farmer's boy. Warne n.d.

Caldecott, Randolph. The fox jumps over the parson's gate. Warne n.d.

Caldecott, Randolph. A frog he would a-wooing go. Warne n.d.

Caldecott, Randolph. Hey diddle diddle picture book and baby bunting. Warne n.d.

Caldecott, Randolph. The house that Jack built. Warne 1878.

Caldecott, Randolph. The Queen of hearts. Warne n.d.

Caldecott, Randolph. Ride a cock horse to Banbury cross & a farmer went trotting upon his grey mare. Warne n.d.

Caldecott, Randolph. The three jovial huntsmen. Warne n.d.

De Angeli, Marguerite. Book of nursery and mother goose rhymes. Doubleday 1954.

De Forest, Charlotte B. The prancing pony. Walker 1968.

Du Bois, William Pene. Mother goose for Christmas. Viking 1973.

Fish, Helen. Four and twenty blackbirds. Lippincott 1937.

I saw a ship a-sailing. Illus. by Janina Domanska. Macmillan 1972.

Lines, Kathleen, ed. Lavender's blue. Watts 1954.

Mother Goose. Brian Wildsmith's mother goose. Watts 1965.

Mother Goose. The mother goose book. Illus. by Alice and Martin Provensen. Random 1976.

Mother Goose. The mother goose treasury. Ed. by Raymond Briggs. Coward 1966.

Mother Goose. The tall book of mother goose. Harper 1942.

The moving adventures of Old Dame Trot and her comical cat. Illus. by Paul Galdone. Mc-Graw-Hill 1973.

Old Mother Hubbard and her dog.   Illus. by Evaline Ness.   Holt 1972.

Old Mother Hubbard and her dog.   Illus. by Paul Galdone.   McGraw
    1960.

Peppe, Rodney.   Cat and mouse.   Holt 1973.

Petersham, Maud.   The rooster crows.   Macmillan 1945.

Sendak, Maurice.   Hector Protector, and as I went over the water.
    Harper 1965.

Taylor, Mark.   Old woman and the pedlar.   Golden Gate 1969.

Three jovial huntsmen.   Illus. by Susan Jeffers.   Bradbury 1973.

Tom, Tom, the piper's son.   Illus. by Paul Galdone.   McGraw 1964.

Watson, Clyde.   Father Fox's pennyrhymes.   Crowell 1971.

Wyndham, Robert.   Chinese mother goose rhymes.   World 1968.

Zemach, Harve.   The speckled hen.   Holt 1966.

W

WEATHER *General*

Fisher, Aileen. I like weather. Crowell 1963.

Sendak, Maurice. Chicken soup with rice. Harper 1962.

Seuss, Dr. Bartholomew and the Oobleck. Random House 1949.

WEATHER *Rain*

Bright, Robert. My red umbrella. Morrow 1959.

Foster, Joanna. Pete's puddle. Harcourt 1969.

Francoise. The big rain. Scribner 1961.

Freeman, Don. A rainbow of my own. Viking 1966.

Garelick, May. Where does the butterfly go when it rains? Addison-
Wesley 1961.

Holl, Adelaide. The rain puddle. Lothrop 1965.

Iwasaki, Chihiro. Staying home alone on a rainy day. McGraw 1968.

Parsons, Ellen. Rainy day together. Harper 1971.

Raskin, Ellen. And it rained. Atheneum 1969.

Ryder, Joanne. A wet and sandy day. Harper 1977.

Scheer, Julian. Rain makes applesauce. Holiday 1964.

Shulevitz, Uri. Rain, rain, rivers. Farrar 1969.

Tresselt, Alvin. Rain drop splash. Lothrop 1946.

Yashima, Taro. Umbrella. Viking 1958.

WEATHER *Snow*

Barry, Robert. Snowman's secret. Macmillan 1975.

Buckley, Helen E. Josie and the snow. Lothrop 1964.

Burton, Virginia Lee. Katy and the big snow. Houghton 1943.

De Regniers, Beatrice S. The snow party. Pantheon 1959.

Freeman, Don. The night the lights went out. Viking 1958. o.p.

Hader, Berta. The big snow. Macmillan 1948.

Hader, Berta. Snow in the city. Macmillan 1963.

Hoban, Russell. Some snow said hello. Harper & Row 1963.

Hoff, Syd. When will it snow? Harper 1971.

Keats, Ezra Jack. The snowy day. Viking 1962.

Kessler, Ethel. The day daddy stayed home. Doubleday 1959, 1971.

Kuskin, Karla. In the flaky, frosty morning. Harper 1969.

Tresselt, Alvin. White snow, bright snow. Lothrop 1947.

Watson, Nancy. Sugar on snow. Viking 1964.

Zion, Gene. The summer snowman. Harper 1955.

WEATHER *Storm*

Edmonds, Walter D. The story of Richard Storm. Little, Brown 1974.

McCloskey, Robert. Time of wonder. Viking 1957.

Skorpen, Liesel Moak. Michael. Harper & Row 1975.

Zolotow, Charlotte. The storm book. Harper 1952.

WEATHER *Sunny*

De Regniers, Beatrice S.   Who likes the sun?   Harcourt 1961.

Ginsburg, Mirra.   How the sun was brought back to the sky.   Macmillan 1975.

Tresselt, Alvin.   Sun up.   Lothrop 1949.

WEATHER *Wind*

Black, Irma Simonton.   Busy winds.   Holiday 1968.

Ets, Marie Hall.   Gilberto and the wind.   Viking 1963.

Garrison, Christian.   Little pieces of the west wind.   Bradbury 1975.

Hutchins, Pat.   The wind blew.   Macmillan 1974.

Mizumura, Kazue.   I see the winds.   Crowell 1966.

Tresselt, Alvin.   Follow the wind.   Lothrop 1950.

WORDLESS

Alexander, Martha. Blackboard bear. Dial 1969.

Alexander, Martha. Bobo's dream. Dial 1970.

Alexander, Martha. Out! Out! Out! Dial 1968.

Alexander, Martha. We never get to do anything. Dial 1970.

Anno, Mitsumasa. Dr. Anno's magical midnight circus. Weatherhill 1972.

Anno, Mitsumasa. Topsy-turvies. Weatherhill 1970.

Aruego, Jose. Look what I can do. Scribner 1971.

Carle, Eric. Do you want to be my friend? Crowell 1971.

Carroll, Ruth. Chimp and the clown. Walck 1968.

Carroll, Ruth. The Christmas kitten. Walck 1970.

Carroll, Ruth. What Whiskers did. Walck 1965.

De Groat, Diane. Alligator's toothache. Crown 1977.

Goodall, John S. Adventures of Paddy Pork. Harcourt 1968. (and other books in the series)

Goodall, John S. Jacko. Harcourt 1972.

Goodall, John S. The midnight adventures of Kelly, Dot and Esmeralda. Atheneum 1973.

Goodall, John S. Shrewbettina's birthday. Harcourt 1970.

Goodall, John S. The surprise picnic. Atheneum 1977.

Hartelius, Margaret A. The chicken's child. Doubleday 1975.

Hoban, Tana. Look again! Macmillan 1971.

Hutchins, Pat. Changes, Changes. Macmillan 1971.

Keats, Ezra Jack. Skates! Watts 1973.

Krahn, Fernando, How Santa Claus had a long and difficult journey delivering his presents. Delacorte 1970.

Krahn, Fernando. Sebastian and the mushroom. Delacorte 1976.

Krahn, Fernando. Who's seen the scissors? Dutton 1975.

Mayer, Mercer. A boy, a dog and a frog. Dial 1967. (and other books in the series)

Mayer, Mercer. Bubble, bubble. Parents' Mag. Pr., 1973.

Schick, Eleanor. Making friends. Macmillan 1969.

Simmons, Ellie. Dog. McKay 1967.

Turkle, Brinton. Deep in the forest. Dutton 1976.

Ueno, Noriko. Elephant buttons. Harper 1973.

Ungerer, Tomi. Snail, where are you? Harper 1962.

Vasiliu, Mircea. What's happening? Day 1970.

Wezel, Peter. The good bird. Harper 1964.

Wezel, Peter. The naughty bird. Follett 1967.

Z

ZOO

Bettinger, Craig.   Follow me, everybody.   Doubleday 1968. o.p.

Carle, Eric.   1, 2, 3 to the zoo.   World 1968.

Hader, Berta.   Lost in the zoo.   Macmillan 1951.

Lippman, Peter.   New at the zoo.   Harper 1969.

Lobel, Arnold.   A zoo for Mister Muster.   Harper 1962.

Munari, Bruno.   Bruno Munari's zoo.   World 1963.

Rice, Eve.   Sam who never forgets.   Greenwillow 1977.

Rojanovsky, Feodor.   Animals in the zoo.   Knopf 1962.

Seuss, Dr.   If I ran the zoo.   Random 1950.

Sharmat, Marjorie.   Gladys told me to meet her here.   Harper 1970.

Unterecker, John.   The dreaming zoo.   Walck 1965.

Ylla.   Look who's talking.   Harper 1962.

bibliography

bibliography

Africa: An annotated list of printed materials suitable for children, selected and annotated by American Library Association and African-American Institute. UNICEF, Information Center on Children's Cultures, 1968.

Behavior Patterns in Children's Books: A bibliography. The Catholic University of America Press, 1966. Includes sections on "little" problems of small children, the value of honesty, the spirit of generosity, the will to work, etc.

The Black Experience in Children's Books: Office of Children's Services, The New York Public Library, 1971.

A Book List For the Jewish Child: Jewish Book Council of America, National Jewish Welfare Board, 1967.

Books for Friendship: A list of books recommended for children. American Friends Service Committee and Anti-Defamation League of B'nai B'rith, 1968. Includes sections on neighbors at home, beliefs into action, holidays and holy days, etc.

Books for Mentally Retarded Children: Public Library of Cincinnati and Hamilton County, 1973. Books for the educable mentally retarded and the trainable mentally retarded.

Books for the Partially Sighted Child: National Council of Teachers of English, "Elementary English", 1965. Lists titles for pre-school to grade 4.

Books That Count: New York State Education Department, Bureau of Elementary Curriculum Development, 1967. Books listed incorporate mathematical principles, and reinforce or develop concepts about number and size.

Books That Help Children Deal With A Hospital Experience: U.S. Department of Health, Education and Welfare, Public Health Service, #HSA 74-5402, 1974. A guide to selecting books for preschool and elementary children.

Books to Build World Friendship: An annotated bibliography of Children's books from pre-school to 8th grade. Oceana Publications, Inc., 1946.

Books to Help Children Adjust to Hospital Situations: Association of Hospital and Institution Libraries, Division of the American Library Association, 1967. Includes sections on cooperation with others, fear and reassurance, loneliness, making new friends, etc.

161

Children's Books of International Interest: American Library Association, 1972. American picture books about children in other countries.

Hello Baby: A booklist for parents and children. Children's Department, Princeton, New Jersey Public Library, 1974. Fiction and nonfiction, ages 2-12, relating to birth of baby and activities for young child with new baby.

Helping Children Through Books: A selected booklist for the seventies. Church and Synagogue Library Association, 1974. Books to help children with problems.

Human Relations: A basic booklist. Madison, Wisconsin, Schools, Department of Curriculum Development, 1965. Books to help children develop attitudes about people of various races and religions.

I Read, You Read, We Read: Library service to the disadvantaged child committee, Children's Services Division, Alabama, 1971. Books, recordings, films and filmstrips of special interest to preschool and younger elementary school children, briefly annotated.

Latin America: An annotated list of materials for children selected by a committee of librarians, teachers, and Latin American specialists in cooperation with the Center for Inter-American Relations. UNICEF, Information Center on Children's Cultures, 1969.

Let's Read Together: books for family enjoyment. American Library Association, 1969. Includes titles on today's youth, family problems, religion, etc.

Literature for Disadvantaged Children: A bibliography. U.S. Department of Health, Education and Welfare, Office of Education, U.S. Government Printing Office, 1968. Disadvantaged is used as a term for children whose experience is limited because of poverty, geographical location (city or rural), or handicap.

Little Miss Muffet Fights Back: Recommended non-sexist books about girls for young readers. Feminists on Children's Media, 1971.

Matching Books to a Child's Needs: Louisiana State University, n.d. Audio-visual materials on adoption, death, friendship, frustrations, etc.; bibliography for Education 114x by Edith Edmonds.

Matching Books to Children: The Human Problems Children Face: "The Instructor", October 1972.

A Multimedia Approach to Children's Literature: Qualitative annotations. American Library Association, 1977. A selective list of films, filmstrips and recordings based on children's books.

Near East and North Africa: An annotated list of materials for children. UNICEF, Information Center on Children's Cultures, 1970.

Notes From a Different Drummer: R.R. Bowker Company, 1977. A guide to juvenile fiction portraying the handicapped.

Personal Problems of Children: Campbell and Hall, 1970. Includes sections on the problems of appearance, new child in the family, the broken home, etc.

A Preliminary Bibliography of Selected Children's Books About American Indians: Association on American Indian Affairs, 1969.

Puerto Rico in Children's Books: New York Public Library, South Bronx Project, 1973. A selected list.

Reading Ladders for Human Relations: American Council on Education, 1972. Includes sections on how it feels to grow up, the individual and the group, etc.

Reading With Your Child Through Age 5: Child Study Association of America, Children's Book Committee, 1972. Includes sections on families, real things, city stories, etc.

Recommended Reading About Children and Family Life: Child Study Association of America, 1970. Children's books about special situations including physical and emotional disability, divorce, death, etc.

Selected Media About The American Indian for Young Children K-3: Commonwealth of Massachusetts, Department of Education, Division of Curriculum and Instruction, Bureau of Curriculum Innovation, 1970.

Stories To Tell To Children: A selected list. Carnegie Library of Pittsburgh, 1974. Includes stories for telling of special interest to preschool children, and an extensive list of stories for holiday programs.

We Build Together: A reader's guide to Negro life and literature for elementary and high school use. National Council of Teachers of English, 1967.

We Read: Selected lists of children's books and recordings. Office of Economic Opportunity, 1966.

The World in Children's Picture Books: Association for Childhood Education International, 1968.